The Seven Spiritual Laws of Superheroes

Harnessing Our Power to Change the World

Deepak Chopra

with Gotham Chopra

HarperOne
An Imprint of HarperCollins*Publishers*

HarperOne

HarperCollins books may be purchased for educational, business, or sales promotional use. For information please write: Special Markets Department, HarperCollins Publishers, 10 East 53rd Street, New York, NY 10022.

HarperCollins website: http://www.harpercollins.com

HarperCollins®, ■®, and HarperOne™ are trademarks of HarperCollins Publishers

FIRST HARPERCOLLINS PAPERBACK EDITION PUBLISHED IN 2012

Library of Congress Cataloging-in-Publication Data is available upon request.
ISBN 978–0–06–205968–0

12 13 14 15 16 RRD(H) 10 9 8 7 6 5 4 3 2 1

CONTENTS

Foreword   v

Introduction   1

The Law of Balance   9

The Law of Transformation   31

The Law of Power   53

The Law of Love   79

The Law of Creativity   97

The Law of Intention   115

The Law of Transcendence   131

Activating the Superhero Brain   155

Superhero Reading List   165

FOREWORD

I read my first comic book when I was about six years old. My father handed it to me with the following instructions: "Here—read this. The most important thing you'll ever learn is how to tell great stories."

Contrary to what may seem obvious, given my name, that comic was not actually *Batman* (Gautam, Gotama, or my anglicized spelling, Gotham, is the original name of the Buddha—how it became Gotham City, I have no idea), and I can attest to the fact that only recently has my father become a fan of the Dark Knight. That first comic was actually a story about Lord Krishna, one of India's most beloved gods.

I. Loved. It.

Through the years, I'd amass more old Indian comics every time my family traveled to our ancestral homeland in India to visit my grandparents who lived there. There were hundreds of those comics that chronicled all the great stories of Indian gods and goddesses, kings and queens, invaders and liberators, warriors and sages, and my cousins and I collected them all. Eventually, as I reached adolescence, I got caught up in the wave of Western comics too—*Batman, Superman, Spider-Man, X-Men,* and all the rest. I studied Alan

Moore and Stan Lee and other visionary thinkers who toiled in the relatively obscure world of comic-book storytelling. Several years ago, I even started a comic-book company with a good friend and rode yet another comic-book wave as countless characters donned their capes and tights and took Hollywood by storm.

All this while, my father was leading a charge, bringing the East to the West, making things like yoga and chai and ideas like karma and mantras part of our everyday vernacular. Sure, I noticed. How could I not? He was on *Oprah*. Elizabeth Taylor and Michael Jackson came to our house for dinner. His bestsellers paid my college tuition.

But then our worlds really started to intersect. In a college film class, I watched *Star Wars* again. "Use the force, Luke . . ." rang a bell. So did Morpheus in *The Matrix*: "The world is an illusion."

More recently, *Heroes, Lost, The Dark Knight*, and many, many more iconic television shows and films spoke to so many of the ideas that have laced my father's books for the past two decades. And it's a two-way street. A couple of years ago when I helped facilitate a discussion at the San Diego Comic-Con between my dad and comic icon Grant Morrison, an audience member asked my father a question about "quantum consciousness." He turned and stared at me with wide eyes and a grin. I knew what he was thinking: He was among his own.

With all that in mind, recently while hanging out with my father (and now as a father myself) and discussing the teetering perch upon which our planet seems to be balanced, I was reminded that he was the one who introduced me to comics in the first place, along with the clear notice that they would play a central part in *the most important thing I'd ever learn*.

This time, I wasn't going to miss the opportunity to find out why.

Gotham Chopra

INTRODUCTION

When my children, Mallika and Gotham, were growing up, we had a ritual every night before they went to sleep. I would tell them a story, usually some sort of mythic tale involving good versus evil, nature, or talking animals. At some point that qualified as a cliff-hanger, where the story reached a climactic stage in which the central character had to confront a nemesis, face some dramatic challenge, or make a critical decision, I'd stop. I'd then ask them to dream up the ending overnight with as much drama as possible. With those instructions, they'd go off to sleep poised for an adventure. In the morning, when they woke up and climbed into our bed, I'd ask them to tell me about their dreams. I'd listen patiently as they narrated the quests they'd been on. I was amazed at their fertile imaginations and the magnificent journeys they went on in the midnight hours. Frequently their stories reminded me of the great myths of humanity—those epic stories of good versus evil, romance and drama, betrayal, loyalty, conflict, conquest, virtue, and vice, many emotions and experiences that they themselves had not yet confronted in their young lives. Were their innocent minds tapping into the deep reservoir of the collective imagination?

The great Swiss psychologist Carl Jung made us aware of the collective unconscious and its archetypal symbols. Myths exist in this "akashic field," or a nonlocal plane of existence, where information, and in this case the collective imagination, is stored and from which it gets re-created generation after generation. Myths are the closest we can come to conceptualizing the nonconceptual—the infinite. They are the highest expression of the finite—of striving to articulate the infinite. These tales are primordial; they capture the transcendent and then cloak it with beginnings, middles, and ends. Often the stories are similar, but take on modern masks and costumes. They have a simple plot and compelling characters and often depict the eternal struggle between good and evil, the sacred and profane, the divine and diabolical. The good guys keep winning, but never really win. The bad guys often lose, but occasionally give the impression that they've won. In truth neither side ever really wins or loses, and the story never ends. This is the dance between creativity and inertia, between evolution and entropy.

Later, as the kids grew up, when I traveled back from my ancestral homeland in India, I'd bring them suitcases full of native comics that retold the great epics of our Indian heritage. This of course further stimulated their imaginations, since the great stories of countless gods and goddesses, emperors and conquerors were so vividly depicted in the pages of those comics. I like to think that all of this played a very strong role in the fact that both Mallika and Gotham have grown up to be great storytellers.

While in high school Gotham was never the strongest student as far as grades go, but his creativity was noticeable, and that trend continued in college, when he attended Columbia University in New York City. As I always had, I chose to focus my support on those areas he was interested in rather than worry about his grades in areas he seemed disinterested in. I encouraged his collegiate explorations in the subjects of comparative religion, literature, and film. Upon graduation, he and his friend Sharad Devarajan conceived the idea of reimagining some of the Indian stories chronicled in those old comic books and bringing them to the world.

Together they started to recruit young writers and artists in India—one of whom is named Jeevan Kang and whose original artwork fills out the following pages. Like Jeevan, these mavericks were mostly young men who otherwise would likely have ended up working as outsourcers for big Western studio conglomerates, but were instead excited by the idea of flexing their creative muscles and dreaming up new characters and stories. Soon Gotham and Sharad approached Sir Richard Branson for investment support, and together they formed a comic-book company called Virgin Comics. Today, after years of building the company with the Virgin group, it is now owned mostly by Gotham and Sharad and is named Liquid Comics (www.liquidcomics.com). Gotham, Sharad, and the creators they have assembled produce great modern myths and are developing their stories beyond the page into digital domains, feature films, video games, and more. Some of their projects are in collaboration with filmmakers like John Woo, Guy Ritchie, Shekhar Kapur, Wes Craven, and others.

This book is an evolution, culmination, and amalgamation of all of the above. In many ways, I see it as a distillation of years' worth of my own ideas, explorations, understanding of consciousness, and mythmaking fused with those of Gotham and a new generation of creators and storytellers. I take great pride in the notion that once again, like so many years ago, I started stories filled with archetypal elements and characters and am listening in as my son and others in partnership with me take them to great new heights. This is consistent with my belief that real, enduring myths and the characters that populate them are never generated by one creator. They are drawn from those universal fields that are the fruit of eons' worth of human dreams, aspirations, fears, and imaginings, and they are in constant transformation and evolution.

This book is the story of modern mythmaking and the creation of new superheroes who will transcend national and ethnic identity. These superheroes are desperately needed to resolve our current crises in a world filled with conflict, terror, war, eco-destruction, and social and economic injustice. The characters and qualities generated and described are special and pioneering; they are the synthesis of my own reflection and, equally important, the understanding of Gotham and his generation, who have been inspired by and have emulated the greatest superheroes, both Eastern and Western, from Buddha to Batman.

The Seven Spiritual Laws of Superheroes was inspired by my book *The Seven Spiritual Laws of Success.* I have tried to pick up on the essence of that book as applied to the next generation of spiritual seekers. This is also a book about my own personal journey as I taught Gotham the superheroes of India and in turn learned from him about the superheroes of America. Over the past few years, both of us have frequently spoken at and participated in the sprawling San Diego Comic-Con in panels with other fantastic mythmakers, including the legendary Stan Lee, the creator of the Marvel Universe, and Grant Morrison, the most prolific writer in the comic-book industry today.

New superheroes must express themselves in the language of our time and speak to a new generation, though they cannot be owned or limited by any of us. We live in perilous times and at a crossroads. On the one hand, we risk our extinction and that of our planet because of the devastating combination of ancient tribal habits and modern technologies that have the ability to obliterate every living being on the planet several times over. On the other hand, we also possess a nervous system through which the universe is becoming self-aware. More than ever, we have the means and insight to create a brave new world in which our current stage of survival of the fittest can evolve to one of survival of the wisest. The road we choose will determine our future. That choice will be shaped by the qualities we aspire to, qualities that we can identify and emulate in some of the great heroes and heroines who have populated the legends and lore of our civilization throughout our time here so far.

It is no coincidence that in our times, superheroes have captured the cultural imagination like never before. Everywhere you look, superheroes and the supernatural have become a dynamic part of our mainstream conversation. Superheroes are imbued with magical powers that challenge the laws of space and time, offering us a vision of a world that can change. Superheroes explore the boundaries of energy and awareness and allow us to better understand ourselves and our potential.

That's why, in my opinion, superheroes can help us save the planet in a very real way. Most important, we can become those superheroes. In the following pages, I attempt to connect the dots between some of the ancient wisdom traditions as I have understood them throughout my life and the costumed superhero characters who fill up the modern mythologies of today. In Batman, I see qualities that resemble those of Buddha. In Superman, surely there are attributes that also define Lord Shiva. Beyond that, though, there are new frontiers I think we need to reach. We have to not only identify in these dozens of characters certain aspirational qualities that already lie dormant in us, but also nurture them with the powerful ingredients of intention, attention, and action, so that we can create a new cast of characters. Those characters are ones who are in touch not only with their sage self but also with their shadow self, and have a deeper understanding of the connectivity of all things. If we succeed, the result will be a profound road map for living to our full potential, discovering the superhero within, and rewriting the story of humanity.

Deepak Chopra

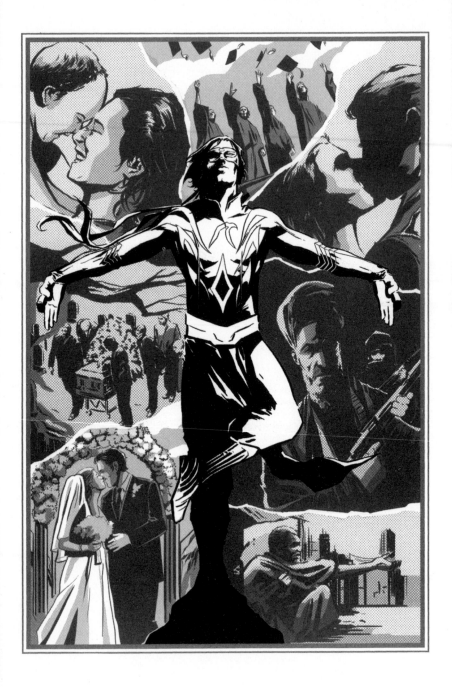

1

THE LAW OF BALANCE

Balance is interaction among being, feeling, thinking, and doing. Superheroes integrate these four core stages of existence amid the turbulence of the world and daily activity and, in doing so, are able to creatively solve every challenge they are faced with and create an atmosphere of empowerment and love wherever they are. As a result, the ideal superhero is a master of martial arts, which at its core is a spiritual discipline.

Recently I have found that asking people who their favorite superhero is, is like asking them who their favorite parent is. It's a question virtually impossible to answer and loaded with great danger. My son informed me that between the two titan comic-book publishers alone—Marvel and DC Comics—there are from five to ten thousand characters to choose from.

"That includes heroes and villains, some of whom switch sides from time to time," he divulged. "Quite often certain heroes will turn destructive, become villainous to the point of self-annihilation." He listed a few examples—Wolverine, the Punisher, the Hulk.

"How about Batman?" I asked, showcasing my limited knowledge of the pantheon, trying to get a bead on what he was talking about.

"He has his moments," Gotham nodded.

"Give me an example," I prodded him.

He contemplated the question for a moment before starting. "They call Batman the Dark Knight, because even though he's a protector of the downtrodden and an upholder of justice, a bringer of light by virtue of being a superhero, it's darkness—shadows and fears—that largely drives him.

"It's the memory of a tortured childhood, shattered by tragedy, the fear of being isolated, and the angst of feeling purposeless that anchor him. No matter what heroics Batman performs, no matter what triumphs he has, his tragic past always lingers and provokes his actions. Even his greatest adversaries—like the Joker or the Riddler—reflect his own contained chaos. They are his own fears and nightmares unchecked and come to life, for within him tremble some of the same qualities that, left to fester, may overwhelm him. He could become them. He exists on the razor's edge, constantly at risk, tempted by darkness, but he rarely falls."

"He's aware of all this?" I asked, impressed.

Gotham nodded. "Batman's anguish drives him."

He was into it now. He kept on going, narrating one of his favorite stories from the vast Batman mythos.

"It's called *War on Crime*. Batman encounters a young boy whose parents have been murdered in a violent attack. To Batman, it's a reminder of his own tragic past when, as a kid and as his alter ego Bruce Wayne, he witnessed the shooting and killing of his parents by a seemingly drug-hungry derelict. Years later Batman now knows all too well the dark choices that faced this boy as he grew up without the stewardship of his parents. Reflecting on the nature of that darkness—from the dank alleyways of Gotham City to its corporate suites so pregnant with greed and gluttony—Batman watches as the young orphan walks a razor-thin line;

a false step can too easily lead to a life of criminality, conflict, and self-annihilation.

"'It's not the moments of tragedy that define our lives,'" Gotham said, citing Batman's famous line from *War on Crime,* "'so much as the choices we make to deal with them.' Pretty powerful, right?" He smiled.

"Yeah," I agreed. "Not bad."

Great superhero stories are our own. They are metaphors for the challenges and conflicts we face in our own lives and the powers—or inner wisdom—we must mine from within in order to overcome those challenges and continuously evolve.

The struggles Batman faces on the streets and in the alleyways of his city are the same ones that we ourselves tackle in our own lives. The setting, the characters, and the plot combine to create grander mythological stories of good versus evil, but the struggles these heroes face echo our own experiences. In our lives they show up as emotional conflicts with those we love and work with, spiritual and ethical dilemmas ignited by the collision of science and spirituality, and existential angst stemming from the ever-evolving technology that surrounds us. All of us, mere mortals, are subject to these torrents of change. So many of us are constantly trying to chase and fit "meaning" into a rigid and static understanding of the world.

But we can learn from the superheroes we have created together. From their trials and triumphs, from their strengths and weaknesses, we can learn how to see our own daily battles play out. If we can harness their skills, we uncover a wealth of knowledge and a guide to living with profound implications for personal and global transformation. These skills are key to maximizing our own potential as individuals and collectively improving the world one action at a time. And the Law of Balance is the only place to begin.

Superheroes know that the only way to resolve any challenge is by going inward. They understand that balance is the key ingredient to identifying any one of their superpowers, flexing it, and then letting it having its maximum effect. There is a saying in the Eastern wisdom traditions that the measure of one's enlightenment is the degree to which one is comfortable with paradox, contradiction, confusion, and ambiguity. Friedrich Nietzsche agreed: "You must have chaos within you to give birth to a dancing star." This is what great superheroes do. They connect with their own awareness and reconcile the pull and push of their lives. They stay centered and act from that place of strength and balance.

Superheroes thrive when there is confusion and chaos, because no matter what madness swirls around them, they remain rooted. They instinctively understand that life is a confluence of meaning, relationships, and context. Superheroes recognize that to find harmony, we must balance all that surrounds us. In short, superheroes balance the forces of light and dark, rage and serenity, and the sacred and profane within themselves and from it forge an identity that is powerful and purposeful.

Balance comes not only from the principal ability to discover equilibrium amid all the opposing forces of the universe, but also from the ability to recognize and harness them. The cosmos itself is a collection of all the forces that have ever existed throughout space and time. Light and dark, good and evil, the divine and the diabolical, sinner and saint, and every other set of conflicting energies that saturates the universe—these are the lifeblood that courses through us and animates our actions. It's the flow and even collision of these forces and energies that generates life itself. The history of human civilization is just another testament to this, depicting contrasts within humanity itself. For every Gandhi, there's a Hitler. For every movement bred in hate that grows and has an impact over time, there's a righteous one that counteracts and contrasts with it. It's this friction and subsequent balance between opposing forces that lays the foundation of our ongoing existence.

We ourselves are an amalgamation of these energies and forces. Have you ever felt so consumed by anger or frustration that you wanted to punch through a wall or throw the remote control across the room? Then you have felt the rage of the Incredible Hulk or Wolverine. Have you ever felt the need for revenge against someone after being wronged? That's the same vengefulness that drives Batman, Daredevil, or the Punisher. If these are familiar emotions, then you have already played out a superhero narrative.

Now let's take it to the next level. How do we consciously maintain balance in ourselves and generate our choices from this domain of awareness? How do we act from a place of thoughtful intention rather than react to the swirl of emotions and demands around us? How do we find peace in our daily lives and have that peace resonate in our actions? How do we ensure our path in life is evolutionary?

The beginning of the answer is by maintaining sobriety. In this case, sobriety means being centered and having total clarity of awareness. Just as Batman foresees the future for that orphan in *War on Crime*, being grounded in sobriety empowers a person to make clear and effective decisions.

Superheroes like Batman never give in to anything that diminishes the quality of their awareness. They do not drift into altered states of consciousness that warp their clarity of mind and body. On the contrary, remaining sober and emotionally fresh and energetic at all times allows them to exist in expanded states of consciousness in which no amount of unrest or turmoil disturbs them for long.

Real experiences of joy, ecstasy, and love can only be had in expanded or higher states of consciousness. These experiences come from being connected with the true Self, the transcendent Self (which we discuss in a later chapter). The characteristics of this transcendent Self are the same as those of nature itself. The natural state of the universe is to be in balance—whether it is our ecology, our seasons, or our individual bodies and their metabolism. When something falls out of equilibrium, nature spontaneously seeks to restore balance in order to continuously evolve. The only thing that can stop this process of natural restoration is when we inhibit it by introducing an artificial toxicity into the system.

Superheroes are anchored in total clarity. Because the clear state is so important to superheroes, they do everything to nurture and sustain it. They integrate habits of good physical and mental health. They cultivate their physical well-being through regular exercise and good nutrition, staying aware of what foods agree with their body and make them feel most energetic. In concert with this, they are at all times alert to their mental well-being. This begins with ensuring that sleep is good and restful and, further, that mind-body coordination remains at all times at an optimum level, best achieved through practices such as martial arts, yoga, meditation, and breathing techniques.

Emotional well-being is equally critical to superheroes' maintenance of peak consciousness. It is sustained through healthy relationships and freedom from emotional toxins, such as hostility, resentment, fear, guilt, and depression. To clarify those toxins:

Hostility is remembered pain and the desire to get even.

Fear is the anticipation of pain in the future.

Guilt is self-directed pain when you blame yourself.

Depression is the depletion of energy as a result of all of the above.

Superheroes remain free of these toxic emotions not by denying emotional pain but by being in touch with it and moving beyond it. They understand that any narrative, including their own, cannot be defined in terms of absolute goodness, for anything that lacks basic contrast—the friction between good and evil, light and darkness—becomes banal and dooms a person to eventual and total inertness. On the contrary, the most dynamic and powerful superheroes (or people) are those who can balance the forces of light and dark in their own being, navigate the shadowy regions of their own fears, rage, and dark emotions, and then channel them into more constructive and compassionate endeavors.

Because of their clarity of awareness, true superheroes take responsibility for all painful experiences without ever playing the role of victim. They are able to get in touch with their pain and feelings by exquisite awareness of bodily sensations. Bodily sensations reflect emotional states. For superheroes, the ability to locate emotions and feelings in the body, define them, express them to themselves without blaming others, share them with close friends, release them through conscious ritual, and move on and celebrate the freedom that comes with not holding on to past experiences of hurt frees them from becoming victim to them. In fact, freedom from emotional toxicity frees up immense energy for superheroes, which they can allocate to their own and their community's evolution.

• • •

With and from this state of awareness, superheroes can integrate the four principal levels of existence—being, feeling, thinking, and doing. Conscious awareness of these levels permeates every intention and action of superheroes and enables them to be their best.

The first level of existence is *being*. It means centered awareness. Like that of superheroes, our goal is find the unshakeable stillness in ourselves amid the turbulence and chaos of the world around us. No matter the madness, stress, and cacophony of activity that rages around us—either physically or emotionally—we must find a way to connect with the stillness that resides within.

The second level of existence is *feeling*. Feeling is being absolutely precise in our actions and not getting distracted by toxic impulses that disempower us, like anger, hostility, retribution, jealousy, and fear. There's ruthlessness to this sort of self-focus. It is not that it is nonempathetic, just that there is disciplined precision to our total awareness of our own feelings. Being in touch with our own emotional awareness ensures that every intention that comes from it also is rooted in emotional balance. Feeling also means excising the need to be right and for self-importance. Superheroes are never self-righteous.

The third level of existence is *thinking*. The highest form of thinking is creativity. This means the revelation that there exists no problem that cannot be solved by creativity. This thinking should be in alignment with our highest ideals and values like truth, goodness, harmony, and spiritual evolution. When choices are deliberated and acted on from this place of emotional centeredness, the outcome will be transformational and positive.

The fourth and final level of existence is *doing*. In many ways, it's the culmination of the first three stages of existence and means emerging from those more reflective stages and being action oriented. The actions of course need to be aligned with our being, feeling, and thinking. This happens spontaneously when we are responsive to feedback, decisive, and willing to take calculated risks. Intuitively, when the moment for action is upon us, we will know what needs to be done, and we'll do it impeccably and with the intention for a greater good, leaving the results to a greater unknown with total detachment.

When these four levels of existence are in harmony with one another, our actions, behavior, and presence demonstrate it. Every part of us—from our own sense of self, interaction with others, and contributions to the world—integrates and balances spontaneously, and the results are real and substantive. Decisions flow effortlessly. Our personal intentions are aligned with nature's basic evolution. They lead us to choices that feel intuitively right and that generate synchronicity or meaningful coincidence. Universal intelligence—or the deeper and all-encompassing intelligence that animates all of nature, including us—flows through us. Our intentions themselves are the intentions of the universe. When we operate from that settled and still sense of self, we meet no resistance that cannot be easily overcome.

In the case of superheroes, they are at their best when

operating from this level of balanced awareness, where their own internal emotions (feeling)—even if fueled by some deep-seated, fiery emotion—are integrated with their levels of being and thinking. The result is super*doing*. Batman is the protector of Gotham City. Superman guards Metropolis. They do what's right at the exact moment in the exact way that is necessary to protect those who need it.

Even superheroes aren't perfect all the time. In fact, characters of great mythology have exhibited epic failures of balance. Like us, in the worst of times, they can be emotional grenades on the brink of detonation. Zeus, king of the gods and the most powerful in the ancient Greek pantheon, was legendary for his wrath and penchant for hurling bolts of lightning at those who irritated him. Lord Shiva, his Indian counterpart, was known as the "destroyer of the universe"; his simple blinking of the eyes once brought about an age of darkness that was akin to the apocalypse.

Or how about an even more familiar "superbeing" who's known for his uncontrollable rage and madness: God himself. All throughout the Old Testament, God is a fiery, genocidal fiend who demands sacrifice from his most devoted followers (like Abraham) and punishes countless others (like Saul) for seemingly innocuous, even questionable, offenses. The fact remains, however, that the vindictive, vitriolic God of the Old Testament is the same as the compassionate, merciful Lord of the New Testament. The wretched, jealous, vindictive, murdering God of the Old Testament is not someone you would even want to have a cup of coffee with, but the new and improved God of the New Testament is powerful and graceful, in charge and nurturing at the same time, and certainly someone you'd be happy to bring home for dinner.

All religious and spiritual mythologies are filled with characters like these—gods and goddesses full of paradox and contradiction, whose anger and wrath know no bounds, but on the flip side whose benevolence and blessings bring about miracles, redemption, and revelation. Why? Because God is as we are. God is, in fact, our highest instinct to know ourselves and a projection of our own consciousness. Like superheroes, his imperfection is our own. His search for balance is our search.

Ram is the ancient superhero at the heart of India's greatest epic, the *Ramayana*. He is the incarnation of God on earth on a quest to rescue his wife, the goddess Sita, from the evil clutches of the demon Lord Ravan. Ravan's physical manifestation reeks of darkness and vice—he has blistering, rotting skin, multiple heads, and a truly gruesome visage. He's kidnapped Sita in the hope that her divinity and fertility may help regenerate not only his being but also the apocalyptic environment in which he exists.

In order to rescue Sita, Ram leads an army against Ravan's demon hordes. But before the apocalyptic battle, Ram's spiritual counselors advise him that, to guarantee victory, he must invoke all the elements and forces of the universe and then harness them, so he can utilize that strength in what will certainly be the fight of his life. In order to do this, Ram's advisers continue, he'll need the most refined scholar with expanded consciousness to lead him through a ritual. This cannot be an ordinary man or even a religious official, but rather someone who actually understands how to invoke the multitude of these forces and has actually done so himself. For Ram, they identify a single qualified being: Ravan. In fact, it should be no real surprise to Ram that his archenemy, the most powerful evil being in all the universe, is what he is because he has mastery over all the elements and forces of the universe.

So Ram does the unthinkable. Before the war, he invites Ravan to do the ritual for him. Ravan comes. Indeed, not only is he the embodiment of all evil; he's also the most knowledgeable being, a master of the seven chakras, the origins of true power, both physical and spiritual. Ravan agrees to do the ritual for Ram with a single condition. Ram is confused, not only because his enemy seems willing to help him but also because he doesn't know what he could possibly offer Ravan in return for his services. The demon already has his wife, Sita. Ram's already lost his kingdom and is about to go to war with the greatest force of evil in the universe. It seems he has little to give.

Ravan smiles. "At the end of our war," he says, "at the penultimate moment, you and I will face off, good versus evil. When that final moment comes, promise me that the arrow that strikes my heart will come directly from you. I want God to kill me. Because in that final blow will be my redemption. Your righteousness will balance my rage. Your sobriety will balance my madness. You will light my shadow."

Ram agrees.

Simply put, the shadow is the diabolical part of our soul. In superhero lore, the shadow often appears as the supervillain, but don't be fooled. In truth, the supervillain is just the superhero who's been sabotaged by an imbalance in the self. Whereas the divine energy within us seeks evolution, creativity, and higher consciousness, the diabolical shadow energy within us is destructive, divisive, and self-sabotaging.

Superheroes combat this with the realization that everyone has a shadow, including themselves. Maintaining that you do not have a shadow is actually denial of it, or standing in total darkness, cut off from the world. If you stand in the light, as superheroes do, then you will always see your shadow. With this awareness, the bright light of higher consciousness can keep an eye on the shadow saboteur.

The shadow rarely backs down. Even when seemingly defeated, it's usually just retreated like a skilled supervillain to regroup and devise a new plan. That's because its nature is to obliterate the conditions in which evolution can occur. So if you ignore your shadow or believe that you've conquered it, it will grow stronger and more aggressive. It will not only embarrass you; it will seek to completely annihilate you. Fallen superheroes have allowed their shadow to become victorious. The equilibrium between the forces of light and those of darkness has been permanently perverted, and the decay of darkness overwhelms. Comic mythology is full of tales that show this—of heroes and heroines corrupted by their own power or infected by their egos.

At one point a dark symbiote latches onto the heroic Spider-Man. The shadow being brings out Spider-Man's darker impulses, making him arrogant, vengeful, and selfish. His iconic red and blue suit even turns black as he literally takes on a shadowy persona. But eventually Spider-Man, through his own awareness, is able to resist these shadow qualities and sheds the symbiote. It then occupies another being and becomes one of Spider-Man's archenemies, known as Venom, forever stalking him and reminding the great superhero of what he could become if he were to give in to his own shadow self.

The shadow is primitive and secretive and lives in shame and guilt, slipping in and out of sight. It hides in the secret passages, dark alleys, and the ghost-filled attics and dungeons of our psyche. Abject conditions such as poverty, poor leadership, an "us versus them" mentality, repression, deprivation, social injustice, torture, self-righteous morality, suppression of desire, fear, and conflict all make the perfect breeding ground for the growth and emergence of the shadow. These rotten and decaying circumstances are familiar from mythological cityscapes ranging from Sodom and Gomorrah to Sin City and Gotham City. But in truth, they really are the lonely and unvisited parts of ourselves. Superheroes are aware of all this and always know how to avoid being in situations that ignite the shadow energy.

Moreover, superheroes recognize their shadows, get in touch with them, even embrace and forgive them, and then put them to creative use. In fact, superheroes understand that, managed right, the shadow can be our best ally. Most people feel guilt and shame when confronting their shadow and hence do their best to lock it away and suppress any sign of it. This of course only antagonizes the shadow and dares it to emerge when least desired. But superheroes are beyond such taboos. They know there would be no experience without contrast—hot and cold, pleasure and pain, darkness and light. In the world of space, time, and causality—or the relative, as we call it—this play of opposites is what drives the evolution of the universe and everything in it.

Having brought awareness to the presence of the shadow and the conditions that can agitate it, superheroes flip things and ask themselves what gift the shadow can actually bring. This gesture alone makes superheroes less judgmental of not only themselves and their shadow but of others, and removes them from the melodrama and sensationalism associated with judging others and engaging in gossip. The result once again is a sobriety that brings superheroes closer to their spiritual energy and creative identity.

In this way, superheroes put the shadow to creative use. For example, if someone has an addictive personality, then that person should channel that addictive energy toward something beneficial—exercise or creative exploration. Some of civilization's most celebrated art, such as that created by the likes of Michelangelo and Picasso, has been the product of the artists' embracing of their shadow and creatively focusing its energy. If your shadow is full of anger or rage, contemplate how that overwhelming energy can be channeled somewhere else and be more productive. In the sobriety of becoming aware of yourself and your shadow, you are now empowered to manage it.

Comic lore and great ancient mythologies are usually set amid harsh circumstances. Whether rotting cityscapes crammed with crime and poverty or imaginative realms filled with demon races and impending doom, it's these worlds that great heroes often enter to do their work. And it's the feud between these forces that makes up the narrative. In the best of those narratives, the feud never really ends, for any story—or character—in which goodness overcomes evil in absolute terms or in which life conquers death for all eternity risks its own extinction. The banality of "ever after" would doom a character or world to eventual stagnation. The quest for balance amid worlds of contradiction, paradox, and conflict is the superhero's journey. It is our journey.

For that reason, balance is the first spiritual law of superheroes. To achieve our quest for peace in our daily lives and aspire toward higher consciousness, finding and maintaining the fragile balance among being, feeling, thinking, and doing is critical. Recognizing and rescuing your shadow from the dungeons of your own psyche—and then putting it to creative use through mindful sobriety—is the most effective and practical way to practice the Law of Balance.

This law, when practiced, has the potential to change the way we think and act. We can step out of the barrage of noise that surrounds us and discover our potential for living in harmony with ourselves and the world. Our actions, decisions, and thoughts become grounded, and we begin to see the world and our place in it from an entirely new perspective. Like a superhero sitting above the earth looking down, we too suddenly gain a new perspective.

The following superhero exercises will nurture balance. Become more mindful of them in your behavior by integrating rituals around them every day; observe them at specific times of the day or for certain timed periods. Eventually they will become part of your normal existence.

1. *Commit to good physical and emotional well-being.* Be mindful of your fitness; integrate some form of regular cardiovascular exercise into your daily routine. Also pay attention to your diet and what you put in your body. Likewise, when it comes to your emotional body, become aware of the toxic

relationships and situations in which you place yourself and gradually remove them from your life.

2. *Understand and maintain a healthy relationship with your shadow.* Identify those qualities in others that create stress, resistance, revulsion, frustration, and anger. Make a list of them and then reflect on their presence in you. The next time you feel one of these destructive emotions percolating, breathe into it and contemplate its origins. Do not become a victim of your emotions. Recognize them and consider how you can channel them into something more constructive.

2

THE LAW OF TRANSFORMATION

Transformation is the true nature of every being
and of the universe itself. Superheroes are able
to recognize their transformational selves and
all the various forces at work within them and
to perceive the world from an infinite number of
perspectives. In doing so, superheroes never face a
conflict or adversary they are intimidated by
or unable to empathize with.

The one fundamental false belief shared by almost all of us is that there are boundaries in the universe. The reason this is not true is because all boundaries are constructed in the mind. Most of us look in the mirror and see in the reflection an image of who we think we are. Perhaps at some subtle level, we know that that image is also an assortment of memories, past experiences both good and bad, and a projection of the person we consider ourselves to be. This reflection reinforces our self-image, which most often results in a continuation of our behavioral patterns and a rigid self-identity that has trouble evolving over time.

Superheroes, however, see a very different reflection. When they look in that mirror, they view their reflection as well as the mechanics that underlie it, which are vastly different. Not only do they see their own past experiences; they also see the future. And not only do they see their own personal past and future; they see yours and mine, their mentors' and protégés', their allies' and adversaries', and everyone else's. In fact, in their own reflection, they see the full conspiracy of the cosmos, full of all of its beauty and ugliness, its sacredness and its profanity, the brightness of its idealism, the darkness of its ego, and the vanity of its own self-awareness.

Superheroes have learned to live without false boundaries between the personal and the universal. Too often we identify only with an ego that drags around a bag of skin and bones. This then becomes a socially conditioned boundary that leads to a limited sense of self.

The real me, the real you, is everything. "I am the universe" is the mantra of superheroes. They look at the trees as their lungs. If the trees didn't breathe, they would not breathe. And if they did not breathe, the trees would not breathe. The trees and the lungs are a unified single process. They understand that the earth recycles as their body, that the rivers and waters are their circulation, that the air is their breath, and that the energy of the sun and stars is also the energy that animates their limbs and powers the pacemaker of their heart and the electricity of their brain.

This is a fact of science. Your body is in dynamic exchange with all living bodies, including plants and animals, and with the earth, air, and water through the acts of breathing, digestion, metabolism, and elimination. We are all members of a single body. Our bodies are also a part of a single energy field, one with the universal energy field. The energy field is also a universal information field that localizes as thoughts through relationships. Our breath is one with the atmosphere of planet earth. One breath, one energy and information field, one body, one mind, and one consciousness. In other words, at the deepest level we are all one.

I relayed all this to Gotham to see how it resonated with his notion of the world of modern comics. He mulled it over briefly and then jumped in.

"I get it. You're talking about Storm from the X-Men. Monsoon rains, blizzard squalls, tornadoes, tsunamis, hurricanes, blinding mists, even solar and cosmic tempests that disrupt the electromagnetism of the world—these are the powers at Storm's fingertips. Storm is like the Greek god Zeus, who hurls lightning bolts at his enemies, or his brother Poseidon, capable of generating tidal waves in the seas over which he rules, or even God in Genesis, who in his disgust over the wickedness of humankind sends a great flood to ruin the earth. Storm's superpower comes from her connection to the universal Self, which is the power of consciousness itself. It is the source of all creation and destruction, the truth at the heart of the universe from which all things emerge and return.

"In one anecdote drawn from the mythos of Storm, an avatar of another superhero named Eternity once inhabited Storm's consciousness. In similar instances with other superheroes, the hosts were not able to survive, overwhelmed by Eternity's literally 'eternal' power. Not so with Storm. Because she is descended from African witch-priestesses who were one with the ecosystems in which they lived, a skill set that Storm nurtured over time and that eventually made her a goddess herself, Storm is able not only to withstand the mental infiltration of Eternity but also to integrate his unboundedness with her own. There's great wisdom in this experiential identity and she knows it: 'There's more to it than simply possessing superpowers. To be [a superhero] means possessing a strength of will—of self-identity—that nothing can subvert.'"

To Storm and most superheroes, the world is like a looking glass. Everywhere they look, even in nature itself, they see themselves. With this realization come the fundamental understanding that boundaries are false and a newfound ability to see through the walls of our self-made limitations. Superheroes understand that all boundaries are conceptual and not based in reality. For example, borders between nations (say, between Canada and the United States, or the United States and Mexico) are a human conceptual idea. There is no line in nature that divides nations or oceans. The earth is a single organism and an expression of the total universe. Every event in space and time is a conspiracy of all events, and every object is also the total universe as a snapshot in space and time. A red rose, with its beautiful fragrance, delicate petals, and thorny stem, is also rainbows and sunshine and earth and water and wind and air and the infinite void and the history of the cosmos since the beginning of time.

Knowing this, superheroes do away with all boundaries. Their sense of identity is not "I am this" or "I am that" but "I am everything and everyone" and "I am the universe." The result is an ability to see the world as whole and to understand the true nature of all that surrounds us. This skill is key to unlocking the potential within ourselves and within the universe. Without it, we will always be limited by a set of beliefs. Once discovered, the Law of Transformation literally changes everything. We begin to tap into an instinctive and intuitive source of wisdom and power that has the ability to transform every day, every interaction, and every moment into a creative and evolutionary moment. When people are connected with their superhero self, in touch with their true essence, they not only have the ability to change the world; they have an obligation to.

Superheroes understand that the moment they label or define themselves, they limit themselves. Consider this. What defines your experience of "I am" or "I exist"? Are not the air, trees, sun, and earth as vital to your existence as your heart, lungs, liver, and kidneys? Could you exist in the absence of any one of them? Your existence and connection to the ecosystem goes beyond elegant words and phrases; it is a true attribute of the grand design of the universe and, more subtly, the unified field of consciousness. Because the true Self is that field of consciousness, superheroes realize that the act of *transformation* is the key to really tapping into and utilizing this awareness.

The ability to practice the Law of Transformation returns you to your essence—an innocent state of being—because it keeps you from being trapped by judgments. This is how artists see the world. They do not look at objects in the world and define them as independent from themselves. A bowl of fruit, a stunning sunset, a breathtaking monument—these things come alive through the artists' interaction with them. Artists bring them to life simply by perceiving them. This is the tangled nature of the universe, and when we realize that everything in our life exists only because of our interaction with it, we draw a great sense of empowerment from it. As a consequence, we are the ones with the power to orchestrate what we do and do not want in our lives.

Transformation is a very real force and active process in our lives. For example, the version of you reading these words right now is not the same version of you who bought this book or who will finish turning the last few pages of it whenever you reach the end. At a basic physical and atomic level, our body is in constant motion, replenishing and reinventing itself. The body is not a structure; it's a process. This year's version of your body is a recycled model of last year's. At the level of molecules and atoms, you are constantly reinventing yourself, which means you have a new skin once a month, a new skeleton every three months, a new stomach lining every five days, and a new liver every six weeks. Your DNA, which holds memories of millions of years, is recycled every six weeks at the level of carbon, hydrogen, oxygen, and nitrogen.

Likewise at an emotional level, we are also constantly changing because of the web of memories, hopes, desires, relationships, and interactions that we find ourselves involved in. Each of them influences us in countless ways, from the metabolic responses they can trigger within us to the choices they may push us toward that alter the course of our lives. Most of us, however, are not aware of this neverending state of change, so that transformation is not active evolution; rather, it waxes and wanes and falls victim to the ebb and flow of our moods and the emotional climate of those we surround ourselves with. That is, we become trapped by the creation of our boundaries. Our actions and beliefs are limited by our perspective. We become convinced of our own inabilities, or that we are in the right, or that the world is somehow out to get us. No matter what the specific boundary is, the end result is that without the Law of Transformation, we are stuck and will always struggle to change.

In spiritual terms, transformation is not only about gaining mindfulness about ourselves but also about combining insight with a greater awareness of the basic connectivity of all things. Transformation then becomes a readiness to see and experience the world from an infinite number of perspectives. It is the ability to *transform* and then see and experience the world not only from one's own individual point of view but from every other perspective as well. Although transformation in the superhero world may reveal itself in overt physical metamorphosis—Bruce Wayne changing into Batman or the character Storm transforming into a lightning storm—in our world it is a great deal more subtle in appearance, but equally powerful in action.

So what does this means in practical terms? How can we integrate into our lives the ability to truly see and experience the world through the perspective of someone else? Super-heroes navigate the cosmos in consciousness. Through their intentions and imagination, they can take quantum leaps to any location in space and time. A quantum leap allows you to move from one location in space and time to another without going through the intervening space.

Try this. Close your eyes and remember yourself as a little child. Instantly you have traveled in time and are now looking at a different body and a different personality. At one point in the past, you identified with this person, but most likely he or she is no more familiar to you today than a stranger. Now close your eyes and envision yourself ten years from now with a different body and different personality, one that has grown in maturity and understanding beyond the one you have today. The same experience occurs.

Now go outside of your own body. Close your eyes and become an eagle in the sky. Imagine what the world might look like from that vantage point, soaring high above in the clouds. Or take on the consciousness of another animal—a snake slithering through the grass or a dolphin frolicking in the ocean. Or another human persona—a warrior bracing for battle, an alchemist tinkering with magic, or a divine being harnessing the forces of the universe. The way in which we perceive the world shapes the way in which we interact with it, the choices we make, and ultimately what we define as real.

There's a saying in the East: "Reality is an act of perception." When we become mindful of that perception, we gain control of our reality. The ability to steer our own perception—or point of view—is the art of shape-shifting, a core quality of superheroes, but also something we are all equipped to do.

Mythology and the comic-book world are filled with shape-shifters. From ancient Greek gods like Zeus, who often changed his form to elude the detection (and wrath) of his wife, Hera, when he was sneaking around behind her back, to werewolves and vampires, who've infiltrated the world of pop culture, to a range of superheroes like the Incredible Hulk and Wolverine, heroes who physically transform themselves are plentiful and perennial.

The act of metamorphosis is a dramatic and popular cinematic vision, but what is its deeper meaning and significance?

Two teenagers, consumed with adolescent curiosity, hormones at work, give in to impulses, and their lips slowly come together. For them, lost in a passionate embrace, feeling the euphoria of young love, time stands still. Until suddenly: terror. The young girl panics when she realizes that her counterpart is wilting in her very grasp. Not from a loss of passion, but the rapid and inexplicable loss of life. Such was the first appearance of the superpowers belonging to the superhero known as Rogue.

Over time, Rogue learns to harness this gift, gaining the

insight that there are no boundaries between her and the person beside her when she lays her hands on him or her. During these moments, she absorbs the memories, emotions, skills, and powers of whomever she is touching. The longer the contact, the longer she will retain these qualities. And if she holds on long enough, they'll be permanent.

Over the course of her superhero career, Rogue bonds with hundreds, even thousands, of others. During one mission, she battles an alien antagonist by harnessing all of the memories, powers, and emotions she's absorbed in her entire superhero history. The alien wilts and dies. The will and power of the collective is more than any single adversary can possibly combat. Alone, one person can achieve greatness. But together, many can shift consciousness entirely.

This anecdote takes transformation to the next level. What you may consider your identity right now is just a role that your consciousness has chosen to play at this particular moment in time. You are not the roles you play; you are the infinite consciousness that has chosen as its destiny to play an infinite number of roles. Superheroes know the distinction between who they are and the roles they play.

This is the difference between a self-image and the Self. The self-image is transient, ephemeral, and impermanent, like a wisp of smoke lost in the air. The Self is eternal, pervasive, all-knowing, and beyond space and time. It does not recognize the boundaries between you and me. My triumph is your triumph. Your tragedy is my tragedy. And this extends beyond you and me. All of what is around you—people, nature, the world at large—is part of your community, your tribe, your society, all of humanity, and the collective ecosystem within which we exist. Superheroes are in tune with this single living and breathing invisible organism that is consciousness itself.

Everything around you exists because of your participation and interaction with it. The moment you stop interacting with anything, show indifference toward it, or even just go through the motions—whether it is a relationship, activity, or object—is the moment it starts to become less relevant to your life and starts to wither away. Ultimately, a passionless approach to anything in life generates banality, boredom, and eventual emotional and even physical death.

In human physiology, the best example is a cancer cell, which is a cell that has stopped reacting to the community of cells and organisms around it. This cellular death clogs the system and ultimately leads to an even broader systemic failure and unavoidable death.

As you will see in the following pages, each of these laws builds on the preceding law. There can be no transformation without balance. When we intend our awareness to be alert, reactive, and in tune to our surroundings without being a prisoner to our past memories or experiences, we once again embrace the wisdom of uncertainty. Each skill we learn leads us farther down the path to harnessing our full potential.

In the process of learning the Law of Transformation, we

gain an emotional, psychological, and spiritual agility that is invigorating and empowering. What most often gets in the way of this fundamental awareness (after all, we are born with it) is the self-image. It's not just our imposing judgment of the world around us (and others in it); it's the way in which we qualify and perceive ourselves and our actions.

Back to the mirror. Consider that reflection that you see staring back. Unless you are already a superhero or enlightened being, what you see is just a perception of who you think you are. By now you may understand that even your own seemingly static reflection is actually just a snapshot of a relentless swirl of biological and psychological transformation raging within you. You are not just what you see, but all the personal moments and memories of your history that have culminated in the present moment, as well as the hopes and dreams you carry forward for who you *want to be*. But even this insight falls short of who you really are, because it's just the self-image in that case that you are looking at. And by defining yourself by your self-image, the result is a repetition of the same behavior patterns over and over again. And especially if the reflection is not something you like, the consequence is poor self-esteem and the perpetuation of a person you yourself do not believe in. The only way to change this is to shift your perspective from seeing the self-image to seeing the Self.

The Self is in touch with the highest ideals of truth and goodness, for both personal and planetary fulfillment. It doesn't qualify itself as good or bad, because it understands that those are both qualities that lie dormant within and that may express themselves at specific moments in time. Most people, however, get trapped in these static moments. Even though instinctively they see the world through the lens of their own being, which is in constant transformation, they only see the dust on the lens. Instead of a sparkly fresh world that is a ceaseless and never-ending soup of energy, they attach themselves to a rigid snapshot of the world they think they see. They look outward and are alternatively fascinated or terrified by things and then generate their reality from that state.

Superheroes do it differently. Because they know themselves to be in a state of constant transformation, they are comfortable with a world that mirrors the same. They live beyond labels. At the level of consciousness, a singular nature exists that is beyond the labels we impose on it. Seeing and experiencing the world from that state of consciousness, superheroes go beyond definitions and their inherent contradictions and are able to act from a place that is absolute in terms of its utility. Their actions are beyond good or bad, divine or diabolical.

Superheroes don't waste time or energy in self-righteous morality or judgment of the moral actions of others. They avoid the "I am right" and "You are wrong" way of thinking, which is ego-based and rooted in an ignorant and limited sense of self. They tread carefully, comfortable with ambiguity and contradiction, but nonjudgmental of the morality of others and discerning in their own actions.

True superheroes act in concert with the world around them. Even what may seem like a destructive act in nature— a forest fire, for example—eventually generates fertility from which a new ecosystem can blossom. Likewise, the very best superheroes work in service to this planetary or social evolution, even if it means personal isolation or performing acts that may be deemed destructive. Grounded in this awareness and free of the judgments imposed by the self-image, superheroes can transport themselves anywhere at all times and know what is happening through the mere act of attention and intention.

Attention localizes the infinite consciousness to a specific point, and intention allows the consciousness to know what's going on with regard to context, meaning, and relationship. This is a form of intelligence called intuition.

Intuition is beyond logic and rationality. It is intelligence that is contextual, relational, and holistic. Intuition is generally perceived to be some sort of alchemy or mystically endowed gift, but really it is the result of the all-knowing awareness practiced by superheroes.

This is the heart of the Law of Transformation. Free from the boundaries that limit our perspective and understanding, we discover that our awareness is the awareness of the universe, our mind is part of the universal. We are able to pause our internal dialogue and in that silence eavesdrop on the mind of the cosmos. Listening to the Self is listening to the universe, which is beyond all space and time. It does not have a win-lose orientation, and its computing ability is limitless and beyond all rational thought. This is the gift of intuition.

When we are able to listen in on the stillness of the universe, we have access to tremendous power, which expresses itself through radiant confidence, charisma, and clarity. Superheroes demonstrate these qualities through their quiet dignity and humility. They are impeccable and authentic in their actions. Even their language—the very words they use to communicate—reflects this understanding of the power of intention. They are honest and genuine, saying what they mean clearly, without duplicity, and aligning their actions with their highest intentions. Superheroes have no need to prove their virtuousness or express their idealism. They don't have to. Their omniscience, omnipotence, and omnipresence are part of everything they do.

Keep in mind that superheroes, like us, are not perfect. At times, they may struggle with their self-image, be concerned with reputation or how others think. But the point is that superheroes are aware of this other dimension and how it is differentiated from the Self. They also have learned the skills to reconcile these intermittent struggles. As a result, superheroes are aware that by aligning with the point of view of their true Self, not just their self-image, they can express magnificence in every moment of their being, thinking, feeling, and doing.

This echoes the principle in the Christian tradition in which God creates humans in his own image, not just physically but also meta-physically. It's akin to great mythologies ancient and modern—from Zeus to Storm—in which gods and goddesses transform themselves into men and women.

Our bodies are made up of a trillion cells (more than the number of stars and planets in the whole Milky Way galaxy), each of which, it's estimated, does about six trillion things a second, and every cell instantly knows what the other cells are doing. This is the magic, mystery, and alchemy of existence. The great Sufi poet Rumi sums it up quite nicely: "Behold! When you see your reflection, you'll be the idol of yourself!"

The Law of Transformation is a critical part of the arsenal of all superheroes, because it enables them, and us, to go beyond everyday empathy and truly perceive the world from an infinite number of perspectives. This reality that you and I see in front of us is simply an agreement between us—a coalition of the willing. When we truly understand that the boundaries between us are conceptual and self-generated, then we are able to go beyond them. To be able to see and take in the world from a place of shared concern and compassion is to open ourselves to the true wonder of the universe, where everyday existence is inspired and every challenge is embraced with confidence and creativity.

In order to discover the practical implications of the Law of Transformation, here are a few specific exercises:

1. *Recognize and question your limiting beliefs,* whatever they are. Almost everyone, other than a superhero,

has limiting beliefs. Understand that all beliefs are limiting. If you have a limiting belief, it will become your reality; for example,

"I will never lose weight . . ."

"I will never be successful . . ."

"I will never attract love . . ."

2. *Self-reflection on the illusionary nature of limiting beliefs sets you free.* Whatever your limiting belief is, ask yourself:

On what basis do I believe this to be true?

Is it true?

What makes me believe it is true?

How does this belief limit my capacity?

How did I get it?

Do I need it?

What would unfold I if were without it?

3. *Expand your boundaries.* The superhero does not identify with a particular body or a particular mind. Recognize the roles you play—parent, spouse, sibling, employee, sports fan, car enthusiast, and so on, but understand that you are the underlying, eternal role-player who wears different masks at different times.

The superhero says, "I am all bodies and all minds. I am the universe." Use the mantra "I am" or "Ah-hum" to remind you of this permanent identity. "I am" is without labels and has the potential for infinite possibilities.

4. *Practice transformation through the art of shape-shifting.* Deconstruct yourself. Let your body and mind dissolve in your imagination into a golden pulsating ball of pure potentiality. From this, emerge in any shape or form and through the consciousness of any being, real or imagined. Become a warrior king and experience what it feels like to be in that consciousness, to look like a warrior king, to walk and speak like one, to behold the world through his eyes and hear the world through his ears. Practice in meditation being the wizard Merlin, the cosmic alchemist Krishna, the young redeemers Jesus or Buddha, the Greek goddess of sexuality and sensuality Aphrodite, or the wisdom goddess Athena. Become the wind or a storm, a tree, an insect, hummingbird, eagle, dolphin, cheetah, leopard, or lion. There is no end to your manifestations, because you are the many in the one.

5. *Experience your light body.* Quiet your mind by observing your breath for a few minutes. Now focus your attention in your body and feel all the sensations as they arise and subside. Slowly introduce the idea

that your body is becoming lighter and more subtle. Instead of a material body, it is becoming a body of light. Keep your awareness all the while in the body with your eyes closed, and now visualize it as that body of pure light with the same shape as your material body. Every time you close your eyes for any reason, experience your light body. Soon you will find your material body actually becoming less heavy, more flexible, and more energized.

3

THE LAW OF POWER

Real power is far beyond muscular might.
Tapping into the force of the universe, superheroes
are connected to the moment and plugged into
the source from which all experience, knowledge,
and existence emerge. The Law of Power enables
superheroes to be immune from criticism, beneath
no one, fearless, and able to empower others
through thoughts and actions.

No matter where you are from, India or Indianapolis, Beijing, Buenos Aires, or Boston, you've heard of Superman. You may not know the details of his origin story or his home planet, Krypton, or be familiar with the thousands of comics that have chronicled his adventures, but you know the name that the giant stylized *S* imprinted on a shield fixed to his chest stands for, and you probably recognize the billowing red cape that flows over his back.

Superman is *the* definitive superhero. He's not just an American pop-cultural icon; he's a global icon. Since his comic conception in June 1938, Superman has appeared in radio serials, television programs, numerous feature films, newspaper comic strips, comic books, graphic novels, serialized novels, and video games. He is the forefather of the modern superhero and a symbol of power across almost all cultures. He stands for achieving the impossible, not just because he is endowed with otherworldly superpowers but also because in his being he represents a strength and supremacy that often transcend those of other superheroes and in fact define the ethos.

Most people associate Superman's power with his classic Greco-Roman features—robust chest, square jaw, and sturdy, thick muscles. He is a Greek god wearing a cape and tights. Beyond that it's his renowned superpowers—the superhuman strength, invulnerability, enhanced senses (like X-ray vision or super-sensitive hearing), and ability to fly—that connote superhero in every way. But Superman's power goes deeper. His real power is the power of presence and the mastery of his senses. But it is not possible to achieve these skills without mastering the Law of Balance and the Law of Transformation.

Superheroes are not prisoners of the known. Everything that is known has already happened. To operate within only the confines of the known creates attachment to certainty, and although this may produce a false sense of comfort and security, it actually inhibits emotional, personal, and spiritual evolution.

The unknown exists in the realm of possibility. In fact, the unknown is by definition a field of infinite potential and is constantly manifesting as the known in every moment of the present. Therefore, the present moment is the junction point between the unknown and the known, between the unmanifest and the manifest. Superheroes are grounded there—in life-centered present-moment awareness. They are able to occasionally glimpse into the unknown, feel comfortable with its uncertainty and infinite potential, and actually channel its power into the present moment. This is very literally the *power of presence*—to be free from both the past and future and have infinite flexibility in every moment as it unfolds. As a result, superheroes understand that the best way to manifest an evolutionary future is to live on the cusp of choiceless awareness.

Choiceless awareness is awareness that allows universal intelligence to effortlessly and spontaneously express itself. Superheroes know how to allow this universal intelligence to flow through them. Think of Olympic athletes, great artists, ballet dancers, musicians, poets, or leaders—ordinary people who elevate themselves to the extraordinary by allowing awareness to flow through them. For athletes, it is when they slip "into the zone" and everything on the playing field or court slows down. They can sense the opponent's next move or envision where the ball may be and put themselves in the best position to strike it. In essence they *become* the game. For ballet dancers, the music fades away, its beats and rhythms merge into those of nature itself, and the dancers become one with the dance. These few examples show people in touch with the primordial energy of consciousness. All of us have the potential to harness this skill and discover the gifts of true power.

In this state, spontaneously making right choices and spontaneously doing right actions are natural impulses. "Spontaneously" in this case means that the choices are not conditioned by the burden of memory or in anticipation of a specific response. For superheroes, this leads to the revelation: "I use memories, but I do not allow memories to use me."

When we allow memories to use us, it is easy to become a victim of them. Many of us have demons hidden away inside that can make progressing on our spiritual or emotional path challenging. Very often these can be ghosts from our past—toxic relationships, abusive experiences, fear of emotional uncertainty—that discourage us from taking on new challenges or wading into new relationships with openness and vulnerability. Our superhero self, however, doesn't get weighed down or discouraged by this uncertainty, but rather embraces it as an opportunity to put creativity to use and to seek redemption in every moment.

When we choose and use memories, but are not burdened by them or attached to their outcome, we become creators. Knowing this, superheroes make spontaneously evolutionary choices. Evolutionary choices are those that are in sync with the cosmos and bring peace, harmony, and love to all who are affected by those choices. Being in alignment with the fundamental forces of the cosmos makes every decision effortless and the results empowering.

Superheroes move and act with grace and power. They know that real power does not require force, but rather finesse, timing, and skillful execution. At their best, superheroes' actions meet no resistance and dispel darkness by bringing the light that shines within them. That light is not righteousness or extreme activism, but rather an instinctive goodness and energy that is born in their innermost being.

If you think about it, you'll likely be able to conjure up a time in your life when for a few moments you took on superhero-like qualities. For me, it happened early on in my medical career when I first came to America in the early

1970s. I didn't have much money, and to make ends meet, having moved to Boston, where rent was rather expensive, I would work multiple shifts at various hospitals, often going long periods without any sleep at all. By day I would do my rounds, seeing patients, filling out charts, and writing prescriptions, but at night I'd moonlight in the emergency room. Medicine was different there. It had an intensity to it and demanded an agility and responsiveness that was unlike any other part of my job or life.

One night I was working the night shift at an inner-city hospital, the neighborhood around which was made up of a predominantly lower-income population. Shortly after midnight on what had been a rather quiet night up until that point, two paramedics burst into the ER with a bloodied woman lying atop a gurney. As was the custom, they yelled out her injuries and condition as they handed the woman off to the nurses and me. It was evident from a rather gruesome wound to the side of her skull that the woman had been shot in the head. I checked her vitals. She had no pulse, her eyes weren't dilated, and she wasn't breathing. Technically she was already dead, and her only chance of "coming back" depended upon whether we were able to resuscitate her. Sadly, gunshots, knife wounds, and other gruesome injuries were not entirely unfamiliar in this part of town. Treating the victims of domestic abuse and gang violence had become an all too regular occurrence for me. However, one glance at the woman revealed an added detail: She was pregnant. Suddenly things became downright frantic.

A woman's womb is a profoundly protective space where, over the course of nine months, an embryo is nurtured, a human physiology and nervous system constructed, and a newborn perfected. A woman's womb is truly one of nature's most overwhelmingly exquisite creations and as such is equipped to withstand enormous amounts of pressure, stress, and turbulence. Even still, any medical practitioner knows that oxygen deprivation can have catastrophic effects on the brain and physiology of a baby and, of course, after a prolonged period can result in death.

Surveying the scene, I instinctively knew that time was running out for the baby. In fact, we had none to spare, so I did what I had to. I jerked the mother off the gurney onto the floor, grabbed a sanitized scalpel from a nearby tray, and plunged it into her abdomen.

Sparing the gory details, within seconds I was pulling a premature baby from its dead mother's womb. One of the nurses grabbed the wailing infant from me, snipped the umbilical cord, and within a few minutes had the baby on a respirator, from which it was getting all the oxygen it needed. I stared at the blood-slicked floor—two techs were removing the woman's body and a janitor was already mopping up the floor. It dawned on me that we had lost one human life that night, but salvaged a new one from the brink of death's abyss.

As was my custom those days, I retreated to the doctors' lounge, where I often unwound with a cigarette and black coffee. But this time I could hardly sit down, let alone keep my hands from shaking. Adrenaline pulsed through me. Reflecting on what had occurred, I was conflicted; I was exhilarated by the glory of having saved a life, but tormented by the gruesome tragedy of the one that was lost.

I knew what I had done in that ER—a perfect combination of knowledge, instinct, self-confidence, precision, and fearlessness—was the product of something very primordial inside me, because, even as the adrenaline started to wear off, I found myself increasingly devastated by the knowledge that the baby I had saved would likely face a very difficult life, never knowing its mother.

Those who have qualities of real power need to wear neither a spandex suit nor a red cape to be recognized. They radiate confidence from within, projecting it outward in their appearance. As a result, power is an integral part of their person, not a feature or trait ascribed to them. They feel no compulsion to flex their muscles, puff out their chest, or declare to the world, "Look at me!" In fact, that type of posturing usually is a cover-up for the exact opposite—a deep-seated insecurity and narcissism that requires constant reassurance.

On the contrary, the truly powerful live in a state of never-ending calm. They are not fearful of the future, but rather comfortable with uncertainty and prepared at all moments with the infinite choices at their disposal provided by the unknown. They do not stew in regret, feel guilt over the past, or get trapped by old conditions and habits. That's not to say they are not thoughtful and reflective, but they're not imprisoned by emotions and circumstances that have already come and gone and cannot be changed. As a result, their body language demonstrates the ease with which they interact with the world. Powerful people are comfortable with themselves, prepared at any given moment for whatever lurks in the very next moment and confident in their ability to react with creativity and grace to every situation. Who among us doesn't want to master this skill?

Although Superman's visage may be familiar to millions, his mythology presented through thousands of comics for the past eighty or so years is vast. I asked Gotham if he had a favorite tale from the sprawling archive.

He responded without hesitation. "Alan Moore's *Whatever Happened to the Man of Tomorrow?*"

Ten years after the last sighting of the iconic superhero Superman, a journalist named Tim Crane is investigating what happened to the planet's once greatest protector. His search reveals that Superman's last stand came against his age-old nemesis Lex Luthor as well as a series of other past rivals by the names of Brainiac, Bizarro, Toyman, Prankster, and others. Fearing great danger from their diabolical schemes, Superman brings some of his close friends—notably Lois Lane—to his famous fortress of solitude, where he believes they will be safe. But even there, danger creeps in, and eventually the infamous league of supervillains murders several of his friends. Enraged by this violence, the loss of his friends, and the threat against the surviving ones, Superman breaks his own treasured code never to kill and wipes out one of the villains. Realizing what he's done, Superman willingly enters a chamber stocked with gold kryptonite (which will fully strip him of his powers) and then remains inside it, as it drifts into the arctic wasteland, where it eventually disappears and it is presumed that Superman dies.

But that's not where the story ends. That's the tale told by Lois (one of the survivors from the fortress attack). When the reporter leaves, Lois's working-class suburbanite husband reveals himself to be none other than Superman himself. His powers gone, he now goes by the name Jordan Eliot and works as a mechanic, perfectly content living out his days as an ordinary husband and father.

"Superman was overrated," he declares. "Too wrapped up in himself. Thought the world couldn't get along without him." Jordan shrugs his shoulders, very much content with his past heroics and his current humdrum.

By his feet, Superman's young son plays with what appears to be a piece of coal. He squeezes his hand around it, and when he opens it, a diamond appears. Ah, hope remains. The boy flashes his father's trademark wink and smile as his parents "live happily ever after."

It's a great allegory. Superman's kryptonite is not actually a strange incandescent green element from an alien planet (as depicted in comics, television series, and movies)—it's his ego. More than just an inflated sense of self, it's actually a misplaced sense of self that ultimately undoes Superman. He'd gotten caught up in his own personal mythology and lost sight of his purpose and deeper connection to the real source of his power. He'd let things become personal and, in doing so, destructive.

As individuals, we coexist with the consciousness around us. The moment we start to see ourselves as separate from it, disconnected from the larger ecosystem of everyone else and our collective evolution, we sabotage our own power. This is the birth of despair, hopelessness, and deceit, and it is a ubiquitous threat—not just in the world of superheroes and supervillains—but in our world as well. The pall of this threat thickens the more we lose sight of our real identity. Power, on the other hand, comes from knowing our real identity. Our real identity is not separate from all that exists. We are entangled as body and mind with all beings. Our minds exchange meaning through relationship and transfer meaning to future generations through culture and education.

Knowing this, superheroes express a longing for the greater good. They have no personal investment in power, and yet they are the embodiment of it. This knowing makes superheroes invincible.

By harnessing true power and recognizing the force of the universe that pulses through us, we can begin to act and think with precision, grace, and empathy. We radiate confidence and strength in all we do.

• • •

This real or true power stems from answering two critical interwoven questions:

Who are you?

What do you want?

Only in knowing who we truly are—beyond the various roles we play in our lives (parent, child, spouse, employee, boss, etc.)—and identifying with that transformational Self, can we begin to answer the question of what it is we truly want to achieve. Most superheroes can answer these questions because, first, they are already in touch with their true Self, which goes beyond their own individual egos, and, second, most of them work toward a greater good in order to achieve a more sustainable and happier world. But, as evidenced by Superman in the prior anecdote, even superheroes can sometimes lose their way.

Think of this in your own context. Many of us lose sight of our real identity by attaching it to material things. We define ourselves by the clothes we wear, the car we drive, or the house we live in. We become consumed with the daily pursuits that cloak our ego—that make it feel alternately destitute (because of a lack of material things) and charged with false bravado and superficial power (because of an accumulation of material things).

In turn, we become disconnected from the deeper part of our self. We forget about that real power, the transformational Self that hides underneath and that is in touch with our highest ideals, both personal and planetary. A lifetime can come and go without our getting in touch with that true part of ourselves and the source of real power. We neglect to ask ourselves what it is that we truly want from our life and, even if we do, most of us fail to really push beyond the simplest answer.

Most people answer the question of what they really want by saying that they desire a higher salary or a nicer car or a better home. Others, perhaps a bit more thoughtful, say they want to send their children to the best schools, surround them with security and resources, and ensure that they have bright futures. But if, like a child, you keep asking them why they want these things, most eventually answer that they want them because they assume that achieving these milestones is what will make them most happy. Happiness, in this case, is a state of fulfillment, calm, security, and esteem. And seeing that those we love are safe, secure, fulfilled, and happy makes us happy. In other words, happiness is the key. It is what we are after, even if we create an elaborate scavenger hunt to achieve it.

Although bigger, more expensive material things may be symbols of achievement and success, and attendance at the best schools or prestigious places of work may offer security, they are false substitutes for real happiness. Material conquests and prestigious badges are antidotes we use against the ills the ego causes us. Happiness itself and the pursuit of it by helping others gain it are qualities of the higher self. By tapping into and listening to our higher selves, we start to understand what it is we truly want. We are reminded that happiness is a state of being best achieved by alternately both giving and receiving it. And that's the core of what great superheroes like Superman do

Superheroes see attachment to the known as a false sense of security and recognize that the striving for security (our traditional understanding of power) is, ironically, the basis of all insecurity. Superheroes do what needs to be done with impeccability and the highest motivation for the greatest good and leave the results to the unknown. Their focus is on the action, not on the fruits of that action.

Superheroes move through life with fluidity, vision, and idealism. They are not held up by minor inconveniences, physical or emotional, and always view the world in a broad and holistic perspective. And it's these qualities and point of view that form the foundation for their so-called superpowers.

As we have discussed, a superpower is a very special ability that results when superheroes connect with their innermost being, which is called the Self. Superheroes realize that this Self of the individual is also the Self of the universe. The ground of their being is the ground of all reality and everything that exists. By acting from this level of being, superheroes are not at the mercy of the environment, but create their own environment.

In classic mythologies, this ground of all reality is often personified as a god figure. Characters like Zeus, Hercules,

Atlas, and, in the Eastern traditions, Lord Vishnu engage in mythical quests in which they utilize their powers to help others overcome obstacles or battle brewing evil. Often they invoke superhuman powers, the elements and forces of nature itself, or mystical qualities in order to bring down their adversaries. All the while, despite their burden of divine grace, they are also deeply connected to us because of their humanity.

In modern comic-book narratives, Wonder Woman and Thor are examples of superheroes who are the literal incarnations of ancient Greek gods. As a result, they carry with them divine responsibilities eons old and stemming from otherworldly realms, and yet they are firmly rooted in a human world, which bonds them to us.

In ancient Greek lore, the god Atlas was actually a Titan and predecessor of Zeus who resisted the new king of the gods. When Zeus and his brothers overcame the Titans, as punishment Zeus forced Atlas to literally carry the weight of the world on his shoulders. The image of Atlas bearing the globe atop his broad shoulders has become iconic through the generations, and it applies to all of us in a very real way. Those who aspire to greatness, to become superheroes themselves, must accept greater responsibility as well. They must understand that fundamental connectivity between the individual Self and the planetary Self. This is no doubt a burden, but also the source of great power and an opportunity to shift consciousness.

Like Zeus in the Greek pantheon, Vishnu is the supreme being in the Hindu tradition responsible for directing the politics of his vast pantheon, but also constantly reincarnating himself as both divine and mortal beings, so that he can help solve a never-ending parade of problems that plague humanity. But it's not just what he does; it is how he does it that elevates him to another level.

What Zeus and Vishnu have in common is not just that they wield great power but how they use it to empower others, shift consciousness, and perpetuate the evolution of their kind. Often in both ancient Indian and Greek mythology, great demons, plagues, or other nemeses will rise from the oceans, be spawned by volcanoes, or be conceived from the desert sands. These dark forces threaten to annihilate humanity, and their mere appearance usually stirs up great panic and chaos. This serves as the hero's call to action; when he recognizes that the planet or its people are threatened, it is a personal threat. There is no barrier between the individual Self and the universal Self, so when the latter comes under attack, the individual Self must rally its defenses and rise to the occasion.

This is the stuff that great mythological and superhero stories are made of. But it has practical application too. When faced with grave challenges, some people respond with fear, while others are emboldened by their fearlessness. And fearlessness is, after all, a quality that stems from comfort with uncertainty. Those who are at ease with uncertainty and not intimidated by the moment rarely feel fear and never allow it to be the predominant emotion on which they base their choices.

What is it in your life that you fear the most? Most people's fears stem from childhood trauma, unresolved feelings of abandonment or vulnerability. Or they fear failure—falling short of expectations in their work or their relationships. Whatever the case, fear is often the greatest impediment to tapping the true source of our power.

Superheroes know this. Green Lantern, the man with no fear; Daredevil, whose father taught him to never fear anything or anyone; and Iron Fist, whose fearlessness defines his lore—all demonstrate the power that comes when we recognize what it is that we fear most, reconcile it, transform it, and then are able to mine our unfiltered true strength. There is tremendous power in fearlessness—the opportunity to authentically experience the world as it is, without preconditions, expectations, or the need to validate every moment by imposing judgment upon it.

Gotham also recently shared with me the story of another superhero who exemplifies the Law of Power. A young man, Matt Murdock, is walking the streets of New York City when he witnesses an old blind man about to step into oncoming traffic. When Murdock knocks the man out of the way, the truck swerves and a canister spills from the trailer. Filled with radioactive material, the canister strikes Murdock in the face and, despite various doctors' best efforts, Murdock loses his sight forever. But although his vision is gone, the rest of his senses seem enhanced. He can sense the world around him is a living, breathing, pulsing organism, his reality a single ongoing experience rather than a predetermined perception. This manifests in a superpower, a built-in radar that forms contours he can detect in the immediate environment around him. Matt Murdock, the man without fear, becomes Daredevil.

Most people are prisoners of their perception; their reality is a false promise built upon a false premise. For them, *seeing is believing*. Not for Daredevil. He's spared that riddle. The unknown is his reality. The unknown lives inside of him. Every moment flows through him, the nexus between now and next (the future). Daredevil takes superpowers to a whole new level—he may not be able to literally see what's right in front of him, but he can literally sense what is around the corner. As he says himself (to another hero, named Bullseye): "You're good, baby. I'll give you that. But me? I'm magic."

Superheroes don't have to understand the mystery of the universe. They *are* the mystery. Their power is internal and, when integrated and understood correctly, expresses itself physically in a visible way. Internal power comes from knowing the true mechanics of the universe, the co-arising interconnectivity of all things. We can only learn how to wield power when we can truly grasp this awareness.

Superheroes' power is the power of the universe. It is singular, infinite, unfiltered, and eternal—where we come from before we are born and where we go when we die, and what resides inside of us silently all through our life.

Close your eyes, and find the silence between your thoughts. That eternal silence is the truth at the heart of creation and is your soul. When we are consistently in touch with it, bonded with it, and understand it as our true essence, then we are at our most powerful. Left in this void, this infinite, absolute void of all existence is a new and fresh opportunity to use the single most powerful force in the universe: the power of love and compassion.

That's the magic that defines you, me, Daredevil, and the rest of his ilk. Whereas Daredevil's power comes from tapping into the subtle awareness that surrounds him at all times, Superman's comes from the eternal raw energy of the sun that fuels his strength and stamina. His power literally comes from being connected to a greater source, or in this case the source of all energy. In turn, it creates a persona that pulses and radiates with confidence, charm, charisma, and clarity. At all times, Superman acts with a quiet dignity and humility, because he has no need to prove to others how virtuous or powerful he is.

Certain personality characteristics become evident when we are in touch with our universal Self.

We are immune to criticism, but responsive to feed-back. This means that on the emotional, psychological, and spiritual levels, we feel neither beneath nor superior to anyone else. This doesn't mean we are arrogant or cocky, but a quiet confidence and dignity radiate from us that result in a fearlessness and readiness to creatively take on any challenge. It also means we are never the victim of self-importance, knowing that all self-importance is a form of self-pity in disguise.

We relinquish the need for approval and control. This means that our actions are independent of the opinions of others and detached from any expectations. We are motivated by our own powerful instincts and their evolutionary outcome, not because we have any expectations for payback.

We empower others by allowing them to be themselves. This means we react to people without preconditions and preconceptions. We accept people for who they are and do not force them to conform to our needs and expectations. In doing so, we empower others to express their full potential as well.

Real power does not belong to you or me. It cannot be contained in the body of a single being or stumbled upon through a few regimented steps. It is *being*. It flows through us when we are connected to the moment, plugged into the deeper source from which all experience, knowledge, and existence emerge and to which they return. It is contained chaos, an act of compassion, grace, empathy, or assistance that you can offer your neighbor at any moment. There is no act of greater power than lifting others up from a moment of despair, leading them from their darkness, and empowering them with hope.

When people truly embrace their superhero self and get in touch with that deeper well of power within, they will spontaneously start to exhibit certain attributes that demonstrate power and charisma. But before that full transformation takes place, we can jump-start the process by placing our attention on specific types of behavior that prompt the emergence of the superhero self.

Authenticity is one of the most important aspects of real power. When it comes to their language, integrity, actions, and even thoughts and intentions, superheroes emphasize authenticity over all else. They are honest and genuine, saying what they mean clearly, without duplicity, and align their actions with their highest intentions.

Intention is another vital quality at the heart of what real power is all about. The Bible has it right in the book of John, which starts with the line, "In the beginning was the Word. . . ." Likewise in the Eastern scriptures, it is believed that *Om* is the primordial sound of the universe—the origin of all creation. The essence of these ideas is that our words have power, because they encapsulate our intentions, which drive our actions. Hence, to become conscious of the words we use is a quality that is very important in encouraging our superhero self.

When we are mindful or thoughtful regarding our words and intentions, our actions will be aligned with the greater good. Simply turning your attention toward the person that you aspire to be will make you gravitate toward that ideal. It's that simple.

We live in very conflicted times, full of jihadists and jingoists who come cloaked wearing moral superiority and righteousness. They lurk behind temptations, in the fruitless pursuit of materialism and the false promise of tribalism, and they steer us back toward our egos, the world of "me" and "mine," while disconnecting us from the profound magic and mystery of the universe around us.

In the lore of superheroes, heroes and villains battle daily for control over the fate of the universe. In real life, our battles are on a smaller scale, but the truth is that a triumphant hero resides in all of us, pregnant with true power and ready to react with precision, grace, compassion, and confidence. All we need to do is let it by becoming present and conscious of ourselves and our feelings. The consequence will be to confront the unknown and then gain the ability to draw power from the wisdom of uncertainty. This is not an intellectual exercise or the start of a deconstructive psychological process. In fact, it can be accomplished in a few simple steps.

In order to cultivate the Law of Power, practice the following principles:

1. *Welcome every day as a new day.* A new day is freedom from the past. Let go of the past and all its resentments, grievances, and guilt. Know that holding on to resentment "is like drinking poison and hoping it will kill your enemy." Know that every choice is a decision between a grievance and a miracle.

2. *Be mindful of any tendency to react impulsively.* When triggered by people or circumstances into a habitual reactive pattern, whether it is anger, stubbornness, fear, or impatience, just stop and keep observing your impulse to react until it fades away.

3. *Do not give in to the luxury of distraction.* Pay attention to what is. Listen and look with the ears and eyes of the flesh. Your body is a computer that plugs into the cosmic computer, or universe, and monitors everything that is happening around you. It gives you signals in the form of comfort and discomfort. Learn to decipher these signals. When feeling discomfort in the body, ask yourself what's going on and listen to your inner voice. The answer is there. When you're making spontaneously evolutionary choices, your body feels comfortable, with no localized sensations of distress, almost unbounded and one with the environment, like a great ballet dancer or athlete. All of this means being a good observer. Listen with your heart. Feel what is going on. Listen

with your soul. Stop and ask the following questions; then allow your responses to be spontaneous:

What am I observing?

What am I feeling?

What is the need of the moment?

4

THE LAW OF LOVE

Love, also known as compassion, stems from a sense of universal being and the experiential understanding that all suffering is connected. Superheroes do not fall victim to the false belief in the existence of a separate self. Practicing compassion, superheroes take on the suffering of others, understand and reconcile it, and then seek creative solutions to conquer it through joy and equanimity.

For superheroes, love is not a mere sentiment or emotion. It is the ultimate truth at the heart of creation.

By now you are already familiar with the central principle that underlies all seven spiritual laws of superheroes—that you are not who you think you are, specifically the singular perspective and personalized history that you carry around in your skin and bones. On the contrary, you are the infinite expanse of awareness that pulses through all living things funneled through your own perspective. You *are* the truth at the heart of creation, and your superpowers are made up of your ability to wield the forces that exist in this awareness.

Love may in fact be the most powerful superpower that superheroes can possibly wield.

"I don't know about that," Gotham replied, when I proposed this to him. He shook his head skeptically. "Extrasensory perception, infinite strength, mastery over the elements, the ability to see through time—I mean, there are a lot of superpowers both simple and esoteric, but love . . . ?" His voice trailed off.

I smiled. "You're thinking about it wrong. I'm not talking about romantic love, of whimsical emotions and affections, which I agree can be fleeting. I'm talking about something else. Something deeper."

Superheroes experience love as the ultimate mystery of all existence. Love remains a mystery to them even when experienced in its total fullness, because they *are* the mystery. Superheroes realize that, as human beings grow in the direction of freedom, there is a progressive expansion in their experience of love.

"Okay . . ." Gotham nodded, intrigued, willing to tread carefully down this path.

I saw my opening and decided to speak his language. I'd prove it to him by citing a superhero story or two. But in this case, I'd not reference any superhero clad in cape and tights, but rather two together who have likely had the most profound effect on human civilization since its origin.

As was often his custom after a day spent in the temple, Jesus retreated to a hill called the Mount of Olives. His disciples regularly followed him, for these were times that Jesus would share thoughts and lessons. But something was different about this evening. After a while, Jesus withdrew from the group, knelt down, and began praying.

According to the gospels, Jesus's posture for this prayer was noticeably different from his regular pose. Usually Jews stood upright, lifting their eyes to the heavens, when praying. Jesus being on his knees suggested an urgency and humility unlike any before.

Jesus then recited a prayer to God: "Father, if you are willing, remove this cup from me; yet, not my will but yours be done."

It was the night before his crucifixion, and Jesus was aware of his fate the following day. Even he felt the burden of his destiny, feared he would not have the will to endure it, and sought God's strength to help fortify his own.

Jesus's last night in the Garden of Gethsemane (the specific location on the Mount of Olives) embodies his willingness to sacrifice his own life for the love of humanity. It's his "growing up" moment and realization of what exactly he must do in order to save his people and be the hero he's destined to be. It is the Law of Love in action—the power that comes from compassion so deep that it demands loving sacrifice.

Jesus sacrificed his life for the sake of humanity. Buddha sacrificed his base instincts to become enlightened. In spiritual traditions, this is the ultimate aim—true spiritual liberation, freedom from the known and the cycle of suffering. Generally in our culture this is envisioned as the monk meditating in a cave or observing a quiet life in a secluded monastery, eventually fading into anonymity. But not for Buddha.

Buddha, or "the enlightened one," as he was known at this stage in his life to his disciples, proposed that there was a step more evolved than even enlightenment, or personal release from suffering. It was to share with others the wisdom gained and the experience of higher guidance, and in doing so elevate them to the same stage. Compassion in action. Love as the ultimate superpower encoded in total self-knowing and self-awareness.

Buddha called those who had evolved to this stage of sharing the ultimate truth bodhisattvas. It should be no surprise that the word *bodhisattva* translates as "heroic-minded one," or in common parlance "superhero."

The great prophets of various faiths certainly qualify as among the most powerful and influential superheroes of all times. Aside from Jesus and Buddha, Moses, Krishna, and Muhammad are a few of the other notable seekers legendary for their leadership, insight, and self-awareness. In all their cases, they understood the principle that true leaders are intimately connected with their followers at an emotional and spiritual level. That connection serves as the root of their powers.

Superheroes don't teach principles or preach dogma; they live the ideals on which they are built. Those ideals—truth and goodness, love and compassion, empathy and philanthropy—are encoded within their being, and every action they take, along with every thought and intention underlying it, is a living expression of their selflessness. Superheroes like Jesus and Buddha are the highest expressions of our civilization, because they are totally and completely self-aware. In knowing that holistic relationship between the individual Self and the greater, all-encompassing Self, they are fully aware of everything and everyone around them at all times.

This spontaneous exchange of energy and emotions is not temporary.

Superheroes do not *feel* compassion when faced with adversity or someone who is suffering. They *are* compassion. To most of us, love and compassion are temporary and highly personalized emotions dictated by a prevailing mood or circumstance. But eventually the empathy fades away when that mood or circumstance changes. Not for superheroes. They perceive these qualities differently; they are in the permanent flow of love and compassion. They do not get swayed by the tide of emotionalism, by seeing poverty or extreme suffering, or by the euphoria of adulation and success. To superheroes, these are all impulses emerging out of a singular energy—the same energy that pulses inside of them. They know that energy to be absolute yet filtered through the experience, memory, and context of a single point of view. With this awareness, superheroes can experience deeply the same emotions as someone else, but react with wisdom, sobriety, and creativity.

Superheroes understand that even violent behavior is a cry for attention and therefore a cry for love. Knowing this, they do not indulge in moral self-righteousness or feel the need to pass judgment. They know that people are doing the best they can from their level of awareness. They don't seek to evangelize or convince others of their point of view. On the contrary, they are effortlessly able to see from others' point of view, evaluate the conditions that make it so, and then seek a creative way forward.

Superheroes realize the ego is lack of love, has only a limited sense of self, leaves no place for real love, and diminishes life. In common language and superhero narratives, this is usually the case for an evil archvillain. In fact, the word "evil" is spelled in the reverse order as "live." Evil is literally the perversion of love, of love lost, and a desperate need to recover it.

Do superheroes fight evil? Yes, they do. But they have no personal stake in this war. Having relinquished all personal investment, superheroes are cosmic warriors who align themselves with the forces of truth, goodness, beauty, compassion, equanimity, and harmony and overwhelm darkness by bringing in light. Even if they face enormous or impossible odds, they understand that it is their implicit responsibility to face the challenges the world presents. Superheroes shed the shackles of hopelessness and accept the problems around them as their own. This is not on account of false bravado, arrogance, or ego-fueled narcissism; it is because superheroes are literally connected to their environment.

Compassion is a living, breathing, organic emotion that vibrates through them and links them to those around them. Superheroes are leaders, and leaders understand themselves and those they are leading to be a single organism. They are intimately connected and aware that in order to evolve, there must be an emotional equilibrium, coordination, and integration between them.

To see the world from others' perspective is to take on their emotional footprint—to comprehend the world through them. This is the true power of love. Compassion, courage, and creativity power superheroes and motivate all of their intentions and actions.

"I've been thinking about it," Gotham announced to me a few days later. "You may be onto something with this love super-power thing." He'd been combing through stacks of comics he kept scattered in his own home as well as in his childhood bedroom, which remains in our house, a testament to a past version of himself. "Let me tell you the story of Silver Surfer."

A young patriotic astronomer named Norrin Radd on his native planet of Zenn-La strikes a deal with an all-powerful cosmic entity named Galactus, who has a voracious appetite for all forms of energy—notably entire planets full of life. In order to save Zenn-La from annihilation, Radd pledges himself to Galactus, promising to be his herald. Galactus empowers Radd with a small bit of his infinite power (known as "Power Cosmic") and charges him with the job of roaming the universe on a surfboard (a childhood fantasy of Radd's and hence the origin of the name Silver Surfer) to find new planets for Galactus to consume.

Initially Silver Surfer is not so great at this charge, identifying only desolate and abandoned planets for his master to consume. Seeing this, Galactus intercedes and tinkers with his herald, removing his sense of discernment, essentially making him morally ambivalent and without regard for the citizens of the universe's many planets and therefore unconcerned with their fate. As a result, Surfer becomes brilliant at his job, identifying countless planets for his mentor to consume and destroy and in the process slaughtering billions. Together, they are a veritable plague across the universe, perpetrating genocide after genocide with nary an emotion.

But things change when Silver Surfer arrives on planet earth's shores. He is confronted by four superheroes (known as the Fantastic Four) and in battling them (along with Galactus, who's arrived to feed on earth's plentiful energy) is moved by their nobility. It sways him more than he could have ever predicted. In an about-face, he defies Galactus, who, beaten for now, flees, but not before he manages to exile Surfer from the rest of the universe, confining him to earth's atmosphere.

Trapped on earth, Surfer begins to fully observe the planet in its entire splendor. Though powerful beyond measure, he lacks a basic understanding of good and evil, sacred and profane, the very paradox of human existence. Surfer meets a blind sculptress and through his interaction with her, and her gentle treatment of him, begins to develop a deep sense of compassion. Fully immersed in the world of humans, Surfer begins to see all of their complexities and contradictions—the evil, cruelty, deception, and despair so prevalent in all the corners of the globe side by side with such incredible beauty, gentleness, kindness, and hopefulness. And now beyond just observing, Surfer takes these latter qualities into his being. He *becomes* them. He's powered by a deep sense of compassion, a superhero of a new ilk whose mission is to tip the scales from injustice and evil toward dignity and goodness.

Doctor Doom and Mephisto (in addition to Galactus) become Silver Surfer's perennial nemeses—devious and treacherous villains constantly scheming to keep the world engaged in eternal Armageddon. But Surfer presses on, embracing the challenge of these adversaries and even converting some of them. Fueled by an inexhaustible sense of compassion toward those suffering, Surfer is a warrior for good across the universe, a true superhero who answers only to the truth of the love pulsing within him. "Now, I ride the Eternal winds once more, and none shall be my master!"

Superheroes like Silver Surfer don't just tap into the qualities of higher consciousness; they embody them. Like the great prophets, their selflessness comprises the highest ideals that we value as a civilization. When they look upon the world and everyone in it, they see themselves and ask, "How can I make things better?"

As we have been discussing, the connection between superheroes—even civilization's greatest prophets—and us is not far-fetched. Scientifically speaking, at this very moment, a million atoms that were once in the body of Jesus Christ or Buddha are inside of you. And it's not just history's wisest prophets; the same can be said of history's most vile villains. In your body right now, if we tracked atoms by radioactive isotopes, you'd be able to find at least a million atoms that traveled through the body of Genghis Khan or Osama bin Laden. A quadrillion atoms have gone through your body that have gone through the bodies of every other living species on planet earth today. It's no metaphor to say that we are all connected; it's an actual truth of existence.

Superheroes understand this at an intuitive level. As a result, they do not perceive the world's problems as separate from their own. Their own personal body is the universal body. Rooted in this awareness, they realize being connected to the Self is being connected to the universe and everyone else in it. The suffering of someone else—anyone else—is their own. This intimacy has its own effect, a restlessness that superheroes cannot ignore.

From a practical perspective, superheroes are a representation of our greatest selves. We created them as models for our behavior. Their ability to be compassionate and to emanate love is very much part of our collective belief system. But more than that, these abilities are an intrinsic aspect of our potential as human beings. We all have the capability to cultivate the Law of Love and see how compassion can change our lives.

No other species has the magnificent potential we do. We are the only one capable of creating Shakespearean poetry, the music of Mozart, delving into the deeper mysteries of the universe, pushing the boundaries of science and technology, asking ourselves the big questions and exploring the frontiers of our own purpose and meaning. The paradox of our existence is that we are also the only species whose members go to war with each other, perpetrate such horrific crimes against one another, institutionalize tribal allegiances (in the name of God), and steer technological and scientific innovations toward the most diabolical means. Superheroes look at this as nothing other than the ceaseless flow of energy, the singularity expressing itself in a multitude of ways. And yet, their response never wavers; they face all challenges and conflicts head-on with humility and integrity. No matter the odds, no matter the enormity of the challenge, true superheroes never back down. They face the future with courage, creativity, and most of all compassion.

Many people interpret this as a call to action, a charge to go out and take on the world's problems through relentless activism. But any sort of militant evangelism will actually have the opposite effect and turn people off. On the contrary, real change is a lot more local. It operates by the principle Mahatma Gandhi taught: "Be the change you want to see in the world." In other words, if you want to increase the circulation of something in the world—in this case compassion, love, or goodness—then *be* the starting point, and it will organically filter into and have an effect on everyone and everything else around you.

An act of compassion can be as simple as offering your neighbor a helping hand or listening to a friend's problems or as subtle as paying a compliment to a stranger or saying a prayer for someone who is suffering. These may seem like very small, even insignificant acts, but they most certainly are not. They activate the power of intention, which leads to tangible results.

There is a catch to all this, which is that in order for all of this to work, the compassion you feel and the offering you make that is born from it have to be genuine and not rooted in any expectation of return. The reality is that when you release good intentions out into the world, they will inevitably come back to you in some form. It's the nature of the universe and works without fail, even if we don't always recognize it. Caring, affection, and appreciation—more subtle ways of demonstrating compassion—should only be offered to someone if they come from an authentic place. But if they do, witness the powerful effect they can have. Those who are the recipients of these energies immediately become more empowered. In other words, they are pushed farther along in their own personal journey toward their own superhero persona. And witness the same in you—how you feel when you offer that love and support to others. It's just another example of dynamic exchange and the power resident in us all.

As you start to integrate these acts and ideas, become mindful of the finer qualities and layers of love in your life and how you can best express them. Superheroes have journeyed in their evolution through different stages of love through the mirror of relationships. They understand that all relationships are a mirror of the self. Let's walk through what the stages of love will look like in our own lives.

The first stage of love that we experience is *attraction and repulsion*. If we are aware, we know that we are attracted to those in whom we find traits that we have, but also want more of. Conversely, we are repelled by those in whom we see traits that we deny or try to suppress in ourselves. Knowing this, we must constantly ask ourselves, "What are the traits that attract me? How can I become them? What are the traits that I am repelled by?" By acknowledging these traits in our own being, we recognize that we too have both good and bad in us.

We now understand that to have negative qualities is not to be flawed, but complete. As a result of this honesty with ourselves, we will begin to radiate a simple, unaffected humanity that makes us natural and therefore more attractive at all times. As we move from the first stage of love to the second stage of love, we acquire a quality called *second attention*. First attention is the quality of seeing what everyone else sees. Second attention, on the other hand, allows us to go beyond appearances and to intuitively understand the deeper layers and contours of every relationship. We only move through this level by cultivating the art of listening and appreciation, which is always sensing the good in others and showing affection in return. This is also deep caring. Second attention allows us to enter the third stage of love, which is *communion*. The truth is that we all have the ability to commune with the souls of others. In communion, we treat everyone as equals and display honesty and integrity in all our interactions.

Communion allows us to enter the fourth stage of love, which is *intimacy with ourselves and others*. When one is intimate with oneself and others, there is comfort with vulnerability, loss of self-importance, present-moment awareness, a sense of timelessness, and complete naturalness. This intimacy leads to the blossoming of nonattachment, where love takes on a dimension beyond the personal. With this nonattachment, we give up the need to control, manipulate, or seduce. Love radiates from us like light from a bonfire, focused on none and denied to none.

In this nonattachment, we will find the path to discovering true passion. This is the unfolding of the masculine and feminine archetypal energies in our own being. The masculine qualities include action, strength, initiative, and power. The feminine qualities unfold as beauty, intuition, nurturing, affection, and tenderness. The exquisite combination of these masculine and feminine energies stokes the fires of passion in our actions, and the impossible becomes possible.

Finally we enter the rare stage of *transcendence*. We experience physical happiness through the delight of sensory experience. This is the realm of mythical ecstasy where we have entered the universal consciousness and feel oneness with the divine. In this state, we have gone beyond knowing or experiencing the Law of Love—we are actually becoming part of it. And we can finally say, "I am the truth, which is love."

The Law of Love is the most powerful gift we can discover. Understand that along any stage of the path above, we will

begin to experience the ways in which compassion transforms our thoughts and actions. In order to immediately
activate this fusion of love and compassion, here are some
practices to ignite you:

1. *Understand that all relationships are a reflection.* Consider
   those people in your life you are attracted to and
   conversely those you are repelled by. List the qualities
   in them that you detect and then identify them in
   yourself. In doing so, you will come to realize that
   everyone in the world is simply sharing your own
   consciousness, and you will lose the need to so easily
   judge others.

2. *Know that people are doing the best they can from their level of
   awareness.* Understanding this idea will lead to your
   being detached and relinquishing the need to control
   others. Accept people for who they are. And at all
   times, be ready to forgive.

3. *Make note of those moments called peak experiences, which are
   your dalliances with the divine.* These are moments of joy
   and transcendence, when the measurement of time
   is lost. These moments most often occur in either
   silent reflection (meditation) or intense activity (yoga,
   rigorous athletics, or sex) when you merge with
   the experience and stop judging or evaluating it or
   yourself. Let these moments become your anchor.

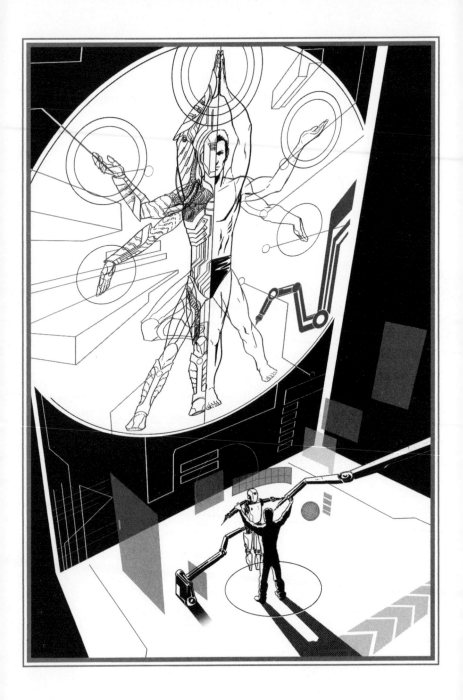

5

THE LAW OF CREATIVITY

Creativity is one of the most practical laws we can harness. It is the principal force that drives all life. Superheroes understand the importance of change and breaking free from destructive and repetitive thoughts and behaviors. Acting on this knowledge, superheroes have the ability to conquer any challenge and obstacle they may face.

Though I've never considered myself particularly religious, my mother was. Every morning, she prayed to the Hindu god Ram for guidance and our family's well-being. As often as she could, she'd rope my younger brother, Sanjiv, and me into her ritual. Indulging her, we'd get down on our knees and bow our heads (and looking at each other out of the corner of our eyes, we'd smirk at one another) while my mother recited familiar-sounding chants. This might've lasted anywhere from ten minutes to half an hour, depending on what exactly my mother was focused on at that time—good grades for my brother and me, good fortune for my father at work, or general well-being for whomever in the neighborhood had managed to earn her favor.

That was really the extent of my formal connection to the gods as a child. Though they were ever present in my life—in India, as with most places in the world, you can hardly walk a block, ride in a taxi, or engage in a conversation without some mention of God or religion—I'd never really looked to the gods for spiritual guidance or evaluation. But although my mother never did convert my brother or me, causing us to join the faithful, she did manage to make us admirers of the gods. I reveled in reading about Ram's exploits and sought out similar types of stories in other cultures—from the great Greek and Roman canons to magnificent Persian tales that echoed the same sort of heroic adventures. Out of all of them, two in particular stood above the rest—Ram, courtesy of my mother's loyal devotion, and Icarus, son of the Greek architect Daedalus. Both were adventurers of the highest order, defiant in many ways of the codes that regulated their divine kind and explorers of frontiers that others only dreamed of.

The story of Icarus starts with his imprisonment. The mighty king Minos has incarcerated Daedalus and Icarus on the island of Crete as punishment for Daedalus's revealing the secrets of the labyrinth, which he'd built for Minos. Desperate to escape, Daedalus puts his creativity to work and, using some feathers and wax, he builds sets of wings for both himself and his son, so they can fly from the labyrinth and the isolated island. But before embarking on their daring journey, Daedalus warns Icarus not to fly too close to the sun, for the wax will melt and the wings will come apart.

Sure enough, as they take flight and make their way, Icarus can't help himself—he peeks at the boundless sky above him, the luminescence of the sun seemingly so close. In the vast expansiveness of all that surrounded him, Icarus has the impulse to test his own self-imposed boundaries, a burning desire inside of him to explore the unknown. Despite his father's warnings, Icarus leaves the slow and steady path and flies higher. And of course, just as his father feared, he comes too close to the sun, and its heat melts the wax that keeps the wings together, sending him into a tailspin that plunges him into the sea.

Through the ages, the story of Icarus has come to be an allegory of the steep price that comes with taking extreme chances or breaking the rules. By defying his father's instructions and literally flying too high, Icarus causes his own demise. Conventional wisdom concludes that life in moderation is the better course.

But there is another way to read this story. Icarus is akin to many other great heroes in ancient myth—Ram, Odysseus, Gilgamesh, to name a few—who forged their own paths, sometimes at great risk. Icarus dared to soar where others never would, to peek inside the heavens and gain its insights. Like Dionysus, who ventured into shadowy forests, defied the gods, and indulged in legendarily amorous games, Icarus was playful and mischievous—a maverick who pushed the boundaries and became the stuff that legends are made of.

In Indian myth, Dionysus's counterpart is Lord Krishna, who as a young man also led amorous trance dances in the forests with the voluptuous cowherd women who worshipped him. Even amid the plentiful other gods, Dionysus and Krishna were looked down upon for violating these taboos, dismissed as lunatics who operated outside of accepted conventions.

That's what the greatest heroes do. They push boundaries, question authority, defy rules, violate protocols, and not only violate taboos but often blitz right through them. In the process, they actually do something very innovative. They look upon every challenge with a creative eye and understand the basic principle espoused by Albert Einstein: "No problem can be solved from the same level of consciousness that created it." Incidentally, thinkers like Albert Einstein, Galileo Galilei, Leonardo da Vinci, Mahatma Gandhi, Amelia Earhart, Thomas Edison, Eleanor Roosevelt, and Martin Luther King Jr. proved this axiom over and over again.

Superheroes exist beyond the world of conventions, thinking outside of the box. They have the ability to solve problems and resolve conflict not simply by *thinking* creatively but by *becoming* creativity itself.

Superheroes recognize their essence as pure creativity. Not only do they have creative solutions for every problem, they can devise situations and circumstances that never existed before. They can activate an entirely new context in which a whole new world can unfold.

Before we proceed, let's start by understanding exactly what creativity is. Creativity is a leap in consciousness that brings new meaning or new context to any situation or problem. New meaning occurs when there is a shift in perspective. When you interpret a problem as an opportunity, that is a shift in meaning. New context results from a shift in the understanding of relationships operating in a situation. A Shakespearean play set in the modern era may produce some totally new insights into social conditions. When both shift, something new and dynamic emerges.

Superheroes are never ruffled no matter what the situation is. Since the word "problem" is not part of their vocabulary, they only see challenges and opportunities. They know that in every adversity there is the seed of something magnificent. Superheroes don't become preoccupied with seeking answers. They don't have use for them. They live the questions and then *gradually move into the answers.* In their world, nothing ever goes wrong. It can't, because they're not attached to any outcome. They accept the world as it unfolds before them, react to it soberly, and then steer it in the direction they want.

The Law of Creativity is a critical part of superheroes' arsenal, because it may in fact be the most practical power they have. On a daily basis, what person does not face challenges, whether with jobs, relationships, finances, or even beliefs? At every turn the world confronts us with decisions that can alter everything that we think defines us. But for the most part, when confronted with a challenge, conflict, or choice, we tend to make the same decision that we have before. We fall back on old habits and routines, at times ignore our better instincts, scared to enter the unknown and contemplate a future of uncertainty.

This is a strange phenomenon, and it's not entirely clear why it happens. As children, most of us can recall times of great wonder and imagination. Building sand castles on the beach, constructing forts with sheets and furniture, or playing out dramas with dolls, teddy bears, plastic soldiers, or Lego people. As we become adults, however, we give up that imagination in favor of the so-called rules and codes of responsibility. Our brains literally lose the capacity to expand, adapt, transform, and evolve. As a result, we doom ourselves to a world of repetition, boredom, and stagnation. We stifle our own evolution and deny ourselves the opportunity to reach our full potential. In storytelling terms, we remove all the suspense, surprise twists, and moments of revelation and redemption from our own narrative. We settle for something far more predictable because it feels safer, even if it dulls the very experience of being human.

Creativity is the principal force that drives all life, evolution, and the mechanics of science. Let's look closer at an example that demonstrates this.

Most people know that caterpillars undergo a process of transformation that results in their becoming butterflies. This transformation begins at the cellular level, prompted by a specific group of cells known as "imaginal cells." Imaginal cells are different from the rest of the caterpillar's cells in that they contain within them the coding and blueprint of something entirely different, namely, a butterfly. These imaginal cells are so different from the rest of the caterpillar's cells, in fact, that they trigger the caterpillar's immune system, which starts to resist the imaginal cells.

But by now the imaginal cells are active. In response to the resistance of the ordinary cells, the imaginal cells start replicating and spreading. Initially the friction between these two sets of cells is almost violent, a tug-of-war to see which set of cells will win out. Cells—like people—gain strength in numbers, so the imaginal cells begin to cluster in order to rally forces and overpower the other, original cells. Jammed together, the imaginal cells begin to share energy and information with one another. As a result, they begin to vibrate and resonate at the same frequency, intensifying their strength. Imagine an army of soldiers rattling their sabers, readying for war. Now comes the rush!

The battle with the normal cells continues, and now, because the imaginal cells are stronger and more powerful in their unified frequency, they begin to overwhelm the normal cells. But somewhere along the line in this process, the normal cells' resistance ceases. The normal cells begin to cluster with the imaginal cells, and they start to take on the same vibration and frequency as the imaginal cells. The chrysalis in which the cells are clustered becomes a humming machine with all of them moving in the same direction. This is the moment when the actual transformation takes place—a caterpillar takes the quantum leap and becomes something entirely new and innovative, a beautiful butterfly.

To the outside eye, this is nothing short of a miracle. It would be like taking your bicycle to the repair shop and, when you return a week later to pick it up, being presented with a jumbo jet. That's how radical nature's creativity is.

Alas, if you were inside the repair shop the whole week, you would have been able to observe the mechanics of the miracle as it proceeded.

Superheroes understand the anatomy of this quantum transformation and recognize that evolution is the mechanics of creation itself. The universe began 13.8 billion years ago, forging itself from nothingness into a small dot, smaller than the period at the end of this sentence. From then on, until this moment right now, the universe has been expanding not only in the direction of infinity but also into complexity and intelligent expressions of itself. The culmination of this process is the human nervous system, where it experiences awareness of its own self. Superheroes look upon this genesis and see themselves as the universe knowing itself through them. They are the eyes of the universe looking at itself.

Right now, right this moment, you have the opportunity to transform your life. Like the single imaginal cell that triggers the metamorphosis of a caterpillar into a butterfly, you too can ignite through your own creativity a radical alteration to your own life and the lives of those around you. It's not a simple mind game of "changing your attitude," but is the result of an actual methodical progression whose steps can be broken down and understood.

Superheroes understand that creativity is not an impulse, but a process. Superheroes become masters of this process by harnessing the power of creativity through nine specific steps. Here's how you can access the Law of Creativity in your life:

1. *Intended outcome.* Have a clear vision of your intended outcome. What do you want to create and manifest in your own life? Imagine your creation—what does it look like? Feel like? Taste like? Smell like? Sound like? Superheroes do not let whimsical notions swim and drift around in their minds; they have living, breathing, multidimensional goals waiting on the threshold of the unmanifest to become manifest. They understand that every intention in this ground state of being is reality waiting to be birthed.

2. *Information gathering.* Gather all the information you need for that particular intended outcome. The intended outcome could be a state of being, such as good health and increased energy, or the acquisition or manifestation of something material. Superheroes understand the meaning of the expression, "Information is power." They know that with the right infusion of energy, attention, and intention, information becomes knowledge. With even more refined intention and attention, that knowledge transforms into wisdom, which places their every action in alignment with all the evolutionary forces of the universe.

3. *Information analysis.* Weigh the pros and cons of every choice made as it relates to the intended outcome. Listen and reflect on what your instincts tell you before acting on anything. See each scenario play

out before you without judgment and evaluation. Superheroes understand that every choice is the doorway to a different future and that an infinite number of futures are available to them. They are able to see the karmic chain of choices that stem from the single one in front of them.

4. *Incubation.* Incubation means letting go, which is best done through meditation. However, there are many forms of meditation—music, dance, sitting meditation, poetry, contact with nature, even sleep. (Superheroes use sleep to their advantage.) During the phase of incubation, superheroes allow the unconscious mind to process information that is relevant to the intended outcome. This unconscious understanding is enhanced when there is mastery in the wisdom of uncertainty and detachment. In other words, incubation is grounded in the present and detached from future expectations. Incubation spontaneously leads to the "ah-hah experience," or insight—a quantum leap in creativity. If the insight is authentic, it leads to inspiration.

5. *Insight.* Insight is the ability to see beyond the known. It occurs when meaning and context have been integrated by superheroes and they can soberly see the sequence of events that results from a single choice. Insight also comes from a place of nonjudgment. Superheroes recognize

that motivation is mental and therefore weak, but inspiration is spiritual, primordial, and therefore unstoppable when it comes from a place that is pure and authentic.

6. *Inspiration.* To be inspired means to be literally "in spirit," or in synchronicity with the greater universe. It is a union between the known and the unknown, a balance and harmony of all the forces in the universe. Superheroes recognize the inherent power of this synergy and maximize the energy it brings to their own being.

7. *Implementation.* When superheroes at last act on inspiration, they do so with finesse, good timing, trust, and intuition. This activation of inspiration happens with ultimate synchronicity with everything in the universe.

8. *Integration.* Once a creation has been implemented, the next step for superheroes is integration, which means taking the experience into a new context and meaning.

9. *Incarnation.* With this new meaning and context, a new incarnation emerges. A new form is born, as is an entirely new situation. Creativity is the culmination of this chain of events—the death of the old and the emergence of something new. What may appear as a totally new situation to others, the superhero knows

to be the product of a process they have catalyzed through their own awareness.

Because the world is a projection of our own personal decisions and internal stories, if we keep making the same choices over and over, repeating the same stories again and again, then the world itself begins to reflect the doomed outlook. Albert Einstein once said that the definition of insanity is "doing the same thing over and over and expecting a different result." Unfortunately the history of human civilization too often reflects this. Our endless wars in pursuit of endless peace are a sad contradiction.

And yet, even amid this maelstrom of madness, every moment reveals a new opportunity for us to reengage the world as we would reenvision it. Here and now, we are presented the option of the creative response. And within that creative response is the coding for a brave new future—the beautiful butterfly waiting to be born from that nervous caterpillar.

"It's like Iron Man," Gotham offered one morning when we were discussing the Law of Creativity.

I was familiar with the name, only because I'd seen advertisements in recent years for the Hollywood movie featuring an apparent hero in a splashy—presumably iron—suit.

When brash, cocky, and brilliant weapons dealer Tony Stark travels to Vietnam to see some of his company's technologies in use, things go horribly wrong. An accident in the form of an exploding bomb has devastating consequences. A piece of shrapnel rips deep into Stark's chest, embedding itself beside his heart. In the ensuing chaos, a Vietnamese warlord also captures him. The warlord will save his life, if Stark puts his prodigious engineering prowess to use and develops a weapon of mass destruction (WMD) for him. Stark's refusal will result in inevitable death.

But Tony Stark is a problem solver. Where others see trouble or insurmountable odds, he sees opportunity and puts his creativity to work. Faced with this dilemma, Stark blazes his own path—literally. He utilizes his skills not to build the WMD but to convert himself into one, creating an iron suit he uses to escape his captivity in a fiery prison break.

When Stark returns home to much pomp and pageantry, he first creates an elaborate magnetic device that ensures his survival, even though it means the shrapnel must remain embedded in his body. He also tinkers with his new invention, the suit made of iron. And now he's faced with another dilemma—whether to streamline and weaponize the iconic iron suit, propelling him to the status of the world's most powerful (not to mention wealthiest) arms baron, or to do away with it entirely. Sure enough, he chooses another option: He makes himself into a powerful superhero whose single mission is to fight evil and injustice wherever on the planet it lurks. He is Iron Man.

• • •

Like all superhero stories, Iron Man's is an exaggerated metaphor for a way of looking at your own life. You don't have to be a weapons manufacturer turned benevolent superhero to flex the superpower of creativity. In fact, it's a lot easier than that. Today, ask yourself one question: How can I be of service?

You don't even need to answer this question, because just in asking it, contemplating it, you will eventually move into the answer, which is right now just a possibility in space and time. If your answer comes from a truly selfless place, without the expectation of anything in return (the Law of Love), then as it reveals itself, you will see in front of you the Law of Creativity in action. You will participate in the act of alchemy (the Law of Transformation) and witness how you yourself have the power to manifest reality through mindful choices. What was just a "potentiality" in space and time will manifest as a reality in your life. "Come out of the circle of time," the poet Rumi says, "and into the circle of love."

As discussed, the Law of Creativity is one of the most practical laws we can learn. Challenges and obstacles face us each day. However, by cultivating creativity we can transform these obstacles into real solutions. In order to become a master of creativity, understand and activate the following principles:

1. *Determine what to get rid of.* What in your life detracts from its quality and is unnecessary? Look clearly

at your life and commit to letting go of whatever is holding you back, including toxic habits, emotions, relationships, substances, and environments.

2. *Practice clarity of vision.* What do you want to create? Ask yourself what you really want, why you really want it, and if manifesting it will serve a higher purpose for humanity.

3. *Follow the nine steps* to accessing your creativity with diligence and detachment.

6

THE LAW OF INTENTION

Intention is the fundamental impulse that activates all action. As such, the Law of Intention is the activating principle behind all other laws. Not distracted by the clutter and cacophony of their own emotions or those of the world itself, superheroes are able to tap into a collective intelligence that reveals itself through confidence, precision, integrity, radiant energy, and charisma.

"You know, Papa," *Gotham started* one morning as we both sipped our coffee, "your story is a lot like Doctor Strange's."

I stared at him blankly. Was this a compliment or something else?

"Do you know the story of Doctor Strange?" he asked curiously.

I shook my head.

"I can tell it to you if you want," he smiled.

Surely this was his plan all along. I nodded, intrigued, and he began.

Dr. Stephen Strange is one of the world's most sought-after physicians. He's rich and powerful, a man with the sharpest surgical skills on the planet, even if his bedside manner is callous and curt. If he has one fault as a doctor, it's that he treats diseases rather than people. To him, every case is a mystery waiting to be solved, and its host (the patient) is just a collateral bystander.

But Doctor Strange's supernova medical career is brought to a screeching halt when an accident causes nerve damage to his precious hands, rendering him unable to hold a scalpel steady in his hands. Utilizing his self-made fortune, Stephen travels the world far and wide in pursuit of a cure, seeking out acclaimed experts every bit his equal in the fields of medicine and science.

When that odyssey proves fruitless, Stephen turns his focus to the fringe, seeking out witch doctors and other medicine men purported to have odd but effective potions or to be capable of performing veritable miracles. But even these adventures eventually turn up nothing.

Virtually broke—financially, emotionally, and spiritually—Stephen culminates his quest in Tibet, where he meets a healer known as the Ancient One. And so begins a whole new journey for Dr. Stephen Strange—one that will go far beyond the parlor trick of restoring his hands' effectiveness to a world of far greater mystery and revelation, one where medicine, menace, miracles, and magic are intertwined and those who know it have a far greater responsibility. In his wisdom and insight into the depths of science and sorcery and the mystery of their tangled truths, Stephen Strange discovers the powers of a hidden mystical realm and becomes a master of intention. He is the Sorcerer Supreme.

Even after Gotham's retelling of the origins of Doctor Strange, I was still not sure how to take his analogy to me. I do confess that my own journey into the fields of medicine, science, mysticism, human potential, and, most important, the exploration of consciousness has been an extraordinary adventure. My understanding of the deeper mechanics of consciousness is plucked from dozens of sources—from ancient Indian Vedanta to modern quantum physics. My curiosity about the nature of the universe and our connection to it has burned inside of me for as long as I can remember. It's why I entered the field of medicine to begin with. And also why I left. All my life I've lived by Einstein's credo, "I want to know how God thinks—everything else is a detail," and at times I've felt on the cusp of revelation akin to that of one of my idols, the Sufi poet Rumi, who says, "I've lived on the lip of insanity, wanting to know reasons. The door opens: I've been knocking from the inside."

In the preceding chapters, I've attempted to outline the most powerful laws I have observed during my odyssey into the understanding of consciousness. As you now know, they all stem from the basic principle of the inseparability of all. This process begins with the Law of Intention, which is not the mystical inexplicable power that many perceive it as, but an actual force in nature with mechanics we can observe, integrate, and practice in our own lives.

Intention is the fundamental impulse that activates all action. Everything in nature is made up of energy and information—from a tree to a flower to a drop of rain to a dolphin or even a human being. What differentiates all of these things is the organization of that energy and information. Embedded in intention is the organizing principle that activates that differentiation. In other words, what separates you from a tree or dolphin is not the substance of your being—which is actually made up of the exact same oxygen, hydrogen, carbon, and nitrogen that make up *everything*—but rather the way those elements have been constructed and the catalyst that ignited that construction, which is intent.

What also differentiates you from everything else in nature is awareness. The human nervous system is built in such a way that we are aware—we can observe our own thoughts, feelings, emotions, beliefs, desires, motives, and instincts. The result is how we experience the world and what shapes our evaluations of it. No other animals on planet earth have the same sophistication that we have or contemplate, ruminate, or analyze their thoughts, feelings, emotions, beliefs, desires, motives, and instincts the way we do. For those who develop mindfulness about all of these impulses and understand the mechanics behind intention, great power—the power of nature itself—can be harnessed.

Superheroes have this power, because they know how to master the power of intention. Intention, free will, and choice are intimately and inseparably linked to each other. For thousands of years philosophers and more recently scientists have debated whether free will or determinism operates in human beings. It is true that most human behavior displays little or no evidence of free will.

Most humans behave as if they are a bundle of conditioned reflexes that are constantly being triggered by people and circumstances to yield predictable outcomes. If you know a person well enough, you know exactly which buttons to push in order to get the response you want.

However, as described above, superheroes realize that the universe has become self-aware in their own being, and thus they are aware that they have within them real power because they have broken the shackles of conditioning. They are free to choose and therefore intend any outcome from the field of infinite possibilities. Superheroes are free of addictions, attachments, and even preferences. They know the best action is the one that comes from consciously made choices.

Intention that is subtle and free from attachment to outcome is the most powerful. The Law of Intention and the Law of Power are closely related, as they both are the means through which the invisible becomes visible and the unmanifest becomes manifest. Without intention, there is no power, and power that is not meaningfully channeled through intention is destructive and can lead to anarchy.

Superheroes also understand that intended outcome orchestrates its own mechanisms. This is based on the principle that intention has infinite organizing power. This means that intention synchronistically organizes the participation of several "possibility waves" from an infinite number of possibility waves to bring about a specific reality.

In the theory of species evolution, some people refer to this as teleology. If you subscribe to this theory, then a giraffe has a long neck, because it intended to reach up to a leaf on a tall tree. A camel has a hump, because it intended to cross the desert with minimal water. And birds have wings, because they intended to fly and soar in the sky.

By knowing that their self is synonymous with the universal Self, superheroes understand that their own intentions also belong to the universe. By applying attention (energy) and then triggering it with intention (transformational impulse) and manifesting their desires, superheroes understand the mechanism that powers all of nature.

Very practically speaking, wherever people pay attention to their life, they see it grow in presence and intensity. This can be either good or bad. More attention, thoughtfulness, and sensitivity in a relationship will bring greater fulfillment, tenderness, and affection. More frustration, resistance, and tension can make a relationship deteriorate and intensify rage, conflict, and vengeance. Removing attention altogether generates indifference and usually instigates a withering process that ultimately results in death. As it relates to a relationship, complete indifference will eventually mean the disintegration of the relationship until it essentially does not exist anymore.

Now introduce intention into the equation. Intention is the desire to bring either thoughtfulness and sensitivity or frustration and resistance to a relationship. What kind of attention is brought makes all the difference in the world how that relationship will unfold. Intention is the transformational catalyst that determines the reality of the future. It is what brings about the manifestation of all energy. In other words, intention on the object of attention determines the outcome by activating and orchestrating all the details that compose the process of transformation. This exquisite dance of consciousness has an unseen elegance to it. A caterpillar intends, which activates the orchestration of its biology and triggers its metamorphosis into a butterfly. All of nature operates like this symphony—from the birds that migrate seasonally, to the plants and crops that come to harvest at a certain time of year, to the animals that hunt and hibernate depending on a particular seasonal cycle. Superheroes recognize these laws of nature, integrate with them, and then utilize them to activate their own intentions and manifest all their desires.

Superheroes also realize that a strong intention in a noisy mind is useless. It is like throwing a big rock into a turbulent ocean. There is no perceptible effect.

On the other hand, a faint or subtle intention, almost subconscious, in a calm and still mind is very powerful. It is like throwing a small pebble in a still pond. There is a clear ripple that spreads across the pond's surface even as the pebble slowly sinks to the bottom of the pond. Superheroes have learned to harness the power of intention by cultivating faint intentions in a centered and still awareness. Their intentions ripple across the vast ocean of consciousness, across space and time, into the whole universe, and bring about their own fulfillment.

The operating mantra for superheroes is "have a faint intention," then "let go and flow," allowing the universe to handle the details. Obstacles are mere opportunities for creativity. This means not losing sight of the intended outcome, while being comfortable with uncertainty along the way. Superheroes don't have to solve all of life's mysteries, because they *are* life's mysteries. With this knowledge, superheroes learn to do less and accomplish more and ultimately do nothing and accomplish everything.

In truth, the power of intention is the principal law that fuels all superheroes, not just Doctor Strange. The goal of all superheroes is to mobilize the forces of good over evil. Even as their understanding and mastery of the other spiritual laws—Balance, Transformation, Power, Love, Creativity, and Transcendence—form the foundation of their expanded awareness, it's intention that is the galvanizing power that ignites their actions.

What does differentiate superheroes when it comes to intention is how they necessarily activate it. Doctor Strange is a man of two worlds, part scientist and part sorcerer. It's the synergy of these two worlds, however, that is the laboratory where his powers are concocted. When facing an evil adversary and required to utilize his powers, Doctor Strange draws them from an invisible world of sorcery he has the ability to access at any time, courtesy of his training by his old mentor. This realm of sorcery is portrayed in comics as a place of powerful invisible forces, where the laws of physics bend and almost anything is possible. Eventually, once he gets the hang of his powers, Doctor Strange is not required to go into any deep meditation in order to travel to the realm of sorcery to retrieve his powers. Instead, he exists very much in this world, interacting with his superhero brothers and sisters and taking on their various archenemies, all the while with the ability to access the realm of sorcery whenever he needs to.

That's the way the power of intention works. When you understand its mechanics and know how to connect with that boundless field of awareness through the act of reflection (which you can refine through the consistent practice of meditation), eventually its presence permeates your life. No longer is the ritual required, because now the field of awareness is always within you, no matter where you are physically. You could be standing in the middle of Times Square in New York City or at the summit of Mount Everest or at the edge of the universe, for that matter: the awareness goes where you go. In this expanse of silence, which is infinitely fertile, planting the seed of intention and harvesting its results is a seamless process.

The best example of this also happens to be the greatest example of a superpower ever exercised: the creation of the universe itself. In the gospel of John, it's described like this: "In the beginning was the Word and the Word was with God." In the ancient Indian scriptures, it's similarly said that Lord Brahma (the Creator) "uttered the word *bhur* and it became the earth; *bhuvah*, and it became the firmament; and *swar*, which became heaven."

Superheroes ever since, from Greek gods to Harry Potter, have cloaked intentions with words in the forms of spells, charms, incantations, prayers, affirmations, and even curses to activate their powers. When Billy Batson said the word "Shazam," he transformed into Captain Marvel and was bestowed the following superpowers:

S   The wisdom of Solomon

H   The strength of Hercules

A   The stamina of Atlas

Z   The power of Zeus

A   The courage of Achilles

M   The speed of Mercury

As a result, there's not much Captain Marvel couldn't do. Like all superheroes with the power of intention, they put the universe on notice. And if those intentions come from a selfless place, they orchestrate their own fulfillment. The universe handles the details.

All superheroes have one-pointed attention. That is, although they may intend things for the future, their attention is always on the present, and that is a critical component to the successful manifestation of intent. One-pointed attention means that, no matter what ebbs and flows of emotion, activity, or anything else occur, the quality of attention is never diluted. It is unbending, unwavering, and fixed in its precision and focus on the intended outcome. This does not mean that it's rigid or incapable of being flexible; in fact, it's quite the opposite.

Superheroes see every challenge along the way to their intended outcome as an opportunity for creativity, but they never lose sight of the outcome. They realize that the journey to any destination is never fixed—that agility, creativity, and nonjudgment provide the pathway to success. But on the pathway itself, they are steadfast in their vision of the destination, never losing the perspective that each step exists within the greater context.

As with the Law of Power, the Law of Intention reveals itself through confidence, precision, radiant energy, and charisma. It also exhibits itself as honesty, integrity, and authenticity. Superheroes realize that every word they utter is truly packed with the power of intention. They choose their words wisely. And they are also wary of using words with destructive qualities. They tend to refrain from profanity, words packed with rage, or redundancy, which of course means I better wrap up this chapter.

The practical qualities of the Law of Intention are extraordinary. We learn focus, clarity of purpose, right action, and how to manifest the life we want. Practicing it grants us direct access to nature's intelligence. It compels us to understand what it is we truly want and then enables us to get it.

• • •

In order to harness this power, you need never consciously force intention. Instead, practice the following:

1. *Seed intention by gently asking questions and then letting answers come.* Sit quietly. Put your attention on your heart. Silence your mind by following your breath and then ask, "What do I want?" Listen to the answer that emerges spontaneously, and you have seeded intention in the depths of consciousness automatically. You need not search for the answer to your question. You need only to ask the question and remain in that stillness for a few moments, after which you leave it alone. Life then spontaneously moves into the answers. This may happen through new situations, circumstances, relationships, and chance encounters or leaps of imagination, insight, or creativity. This is the magic of consciousness.

2. *Never seed intention selfishly or forcibly.* Like a good gardener, you plant the seed by asking a question, and through deep listening you leave it alone. Good gardeners plant the seed and nourish it with water. They do not dig up the ground every day to see how it is doing. So too you plant the seed in your heart and nourish it through the practice of stillness and silence, knowing that it is not only planted, but steadily germinating.

3. *Detach from outcome.* Good gardeners know that the seed will sprout when the season is right. So too your intentions will manifest when the season is right. In every seed there is the promise of thousands of gardens, and so too in every question there is the promise of thousands of manifestations. Superheroes trust themselves and never doubt. If and when there is doubt, they doubt the doubt. The mantra for orchestrating the power of intention is: "Intend, detach, let go, and flow."

7

THE LAW OF TRANSCENDENCE

The Law of Transcendence lies at the very core of who superheroes really are, who we truly are. The ability to access the transcendent is the first step toward knowing yourself and reaching your full potential. With this ability, superheroes can go inward, beyond the secret passageways and ghost-filled attics of the mind into pure silence, or Being. Superheroes need not look at the world, see its chaos, and reel back from it; instead, with the Law of Transcendence superheroes confront the chaos and understand that they are both citizens of that chaos and masters of it.

Since my mother was a quasi devotee of the Indian god Ram, the stories about his many adventures were omnipresent in my life growing up in India. Ram's status in the vast pantheon of Indian gods is very high, because people can relate to him. Although he is divine in origin, his disposition and daily toils are decidedly human. Ram's mortal duties dominate his lengthy mythology, in which he plays the roles of husband, brother, father, and leader, and at times struggles with each of them. His epic quest to rescue his wife, Sita, from the clutches of the demon Lord Ravan is the most iconic story in his mythology, a sprawling narrative full of action, drama, tragedy, triumph, faith, fraternity, love, romance, betrayal, and more.

My favorite Ram story, however, is a lot less spectacular—at least on the surface. It takes place when Ram is still a young boy, the crown prince of the kingdom in which he lives. Seeing that his son feels dejected over the burdens he will one day inherit as the heir to the throne, Ram's father, the king, dispatches the boy to the forest to seek out the great sage Vasishta. He knows that Vasishta can teach his boy the ways of the world. Ram dutifully follows his father's instructions and, after a few days spent making his way through the thick forest, comes across Vasishta, who lives in a small cave, spending most of his time in deep meditation.

Ram recognizes the elder and falls to his knees. He lowers his head submissively and asks Vasishta to be his teacher. The old sage looks upon the boy and instantly sees the divine in him. He roars with laughter and tells Ram to get up.

"You're a god—what could an old man like me possibly teach you?!" Vasishta exclaims.

Ram stays down, but lifts his head and stares at Vasishta respectfully. "Please, sir, even a god needs a teacher. I need to be reminded of who I am."

Vasishta smiles. He agrees to be Ram's teacher. Some say that the ensuing dialogue between Ram and his guru lasted years. Some say decades, and others say centuries. Some believe that the dialogue is still going on between the two—and that the existence of the cosmos itself is the substance of that conversation.

There is a record of some portion of the conversation, an ancient scripture called the *Yoga Vasishta*. In Western culture, yoga has come to be known as an exercise that demands both balance and flexibility, but the true meaning of the word is "spiritual discipline." The goal of all spiritual discipline and the various yogas (bhakti, gyan, kama, karma, etc.) is the true understanding of consciousness. So the *Yoga Vasishta* is really a treatise between the god and his teacher on the nature of consciousness. It's a handbook for Ram, a manual that at its core instructs him to go back within himself to uncover his soul and seek out all the deeper truths of existence. Through it, the god literally is reminded of his true identity and through that comes to know the true nature of everything. Perhaps the most famous passage from the *Yoga Vasishta* reads: "I am that. You are that. All this is that. That alone is." If you truly understand these words, you understand everything there is to be understood.

The Law of Transcendence lies at the very core of who superheroes really are, who we truly are. It's less a power to be wielded or even a catalyst that spurs some exotic superpower. It is a grounding in the basic nature of existence, the foundation on which everything else is built. It is also the most spiritual quality of all, something we will dive deeply into as this chapter proceeds.

Owen Reece, a nerdy scientist, accidentally creates a superhero when he accesses a parallel reality known only as Beyond. Elements and forces of this realm begin to coalesce around a single being who will eventually be known as Beyonder. This "energy being" is initially beyond male or female, good or evil, or even heroic or villainous status, but gradually gains sentience and an isolated awareness or point of view. Still, even while Beyonder begins to engage in more common superhero conflicts—taking on supervillains and meeting the challenges presented in the world of humans—he forever retains that awareness of the great *beyond* and the attributes of pure potentiality, expanded consciousness, and higher guidance that compose it. Those qualities transcend the duality and paradox in which most humans are imprisoned and endow Beyonder with a superpower that qualifies as the ultimate one and origin of all the rest.

The moment Gotham shared the story of Beyonder with me, I liked it. Not only because Beyonder himself is such a great metaphor for the concept of the transcendent, but also because his origin story was so organically bound up with a scientific experiment gone awry. It is at the nexus of the spiritual and the scientific that the transcendent really resides.

Everyday reality is composed of objects existing in space and time. These objects have distinct boundaries. They are material. They are impermanent. They are subject to decay, and they experience the flow of linear time in which there are fixed cause-and-effect relationships. These objects are observed by conscious beings that have physical bodies. These conscious beings are all forms of life, from insects to human beings, with human beings at the top of the hierarchy. What distinguishes humans from all the other living beings is that we have nervous systems that allow us to be self-aware.

Superheroes understand that the material level of existence is an illusion, as it is a projection of the deeper levels. Underneath the material is the level of energy. And underneath the level of energy is the deepest level of intelligence and consciousness. A thought begins in consciousness, becomes energy as speech and action, and ultimately manifests as material reality in the form of a new experience in the world of matter.

As we have seen, superheroes realize that all material objects in the whole universe are part of an unbounded field of energy that permeates the entire universe. Superheroes' bodies and minds are part of this field of energy, and therefore they have the ability to tap into this unlimited reservoir of energy, making themselves all-powerful.

The level of existence underneath the world of objects and the field of energy is the most important and the source of all existence. This, as we have already discussed, is the Self. The Self is a field of transcendent consciousness. "Transcendent" means not existing in space and time and therefore eternal. The Self has no beginning in time, no ending in time, and no edges in space. Consciousness is its real name. The same way that DNA differentiates into my eyes, nose, hair, skin, liver, spleen, kidneys, and all the various wonderful parts that make up my body, consciousness also differentiates into the parts of our total reality. What I see, hear, smell, taste, and touch, my moods and emotions, my behavior and interactions, and the relationships that emerge from these interactions—these are all differentiated aspects of consciousness. They may appear as distinct things, but they are not.

This transcendent field is also self-aware. It is both the field and the knower of the field. At this level, space, time, energy, and information all resolve into what is called the singularity. In other words, they all become one. Being one, they do not exist as space, time, energy, information, or objects. They exist as pure possibility or pure potential. This level of existence is the immeasurable all that was, all that is, and all that will be. Superheroes know this field of infinite possibilities to be their true identity and can access it at any time and in any circumstance. Superheroes do this by remaining centered and living in possibility at all times.

What I have described above in somewhat technical terms sometimes goes by a different name, a superhero who alternatively inspires awe or creates discomfort depending on your own point of view. That name is God. If you define God as a father figure in flowing robes sitting in the clouds, then my description is not the God for you. And if you are uncomfortable with the idea of God entirely, then you can just use the phrase "acausal, nonlocal, quantum-mechanical interrelatedness" to identify this transcendent state of awareness. "Acausal," because it is without cause; "nonlocal," because it transcends space and time; "quantum-mechanical," because it's a very fundamental level of existence; and "interrelated," because every part of it is interrelated and codependent on every other part.

Whatever you want to call it, this is the world where superheroes lurk and where we find the terms and ideas they attempt to make accessible through their own anatomy and being. Done right, great myths produce great metaphors. And there are no greater myths than the ones we create about our most idealized characters—from Beyonder to Batman to Buddha, Iron Man to Icarus, Jean Grey to Jesus.

Jean Grey—a character Gotham shared with me—belongs to a special group of superheroes who, in my mind, like Beyonder, really "get it." Jean Grey is a powerful telepath and member of the iconic X-Men team of superheroes. During an operation, in order to save other members of her team who have been abducted by Sentinels and imprisoned in outer space, Jean volunteers to pilot the craft used to rescue them. Though the mission is successful, Jean Grey cannot withstand the radiation she's exposed to during the daring escape. Even though she's aware of her deathly fate, she's steadfast and sacrifices herself for the survival of the team.

But as she's dying, a cosmic entity known as the Phoenix Force appears. Jean Grey communes with it and merges into it. No longer her individual Self, she acquires the new code name Phoenix. In this new guise, she takes on the attributes of the cosmos, becoming a being of infinite power, pure awareness, and unbounded potential. No longer can she be contained within the body of a single being. On the contrary, she has gained insight into the nature of consciousness itself—beyond good and evil, sacred and profane, divine and diabolical. She is the infinite, eternal, nonlocal, indivisible, underlying equilibrium of all, rooted in every being and everything. As is said of God himself in the Holy Bible, she is the "Alpha and the Omega, the first and the last, the beginning and end." Or as Lord Krishna declares on the battlefield of Kurukshetra, she is "time inexhaustible, the creator whose faces are in all directions."

The greatest superheroes like Jean Grey and Beyonder hold pieces of the infinite expanse of consciousness inside them. They are in touch with that domain of awareness that is beyond measurement and is pure potentiality embodied. Their consciousness is pure consciousness, a field of all possibilities and infinite creativity. From this state of being, they operate with choiceless awareness, and every decision they make is in concert with the universe. They understand that the battles they wage and the struggles they engage in against even their greatest enemies are conflicts within themselves, the ceaseless ebb and flow between the light and dark energies of their own being.

I realize that many of the ideas I am expressing here are echoes of ones articulated in prior chapters. That's no accident. The truth is that all of the seven laws of superheroes are inextricably linked, because they stem from a singular premise—that reality itself is a projection of a single intelligence that underlies all existence. It's worth repeating over and over again, because it is the principle through which everything else can be understood and experienced. Although it is indeed an act of intellectual agility to fully process the notion of a field of infinite awareness from which *everything* emanates, the truth is that you already know it. You are an expression of it, and its essence is ceaselessly pulsating through you. I'd like to come back to this revelation through another route, exploring the intricacies of the transcendent, how we naturally reflect it, and also how we move through it to reach its greatest expression.

A human body can think thoughts, play a piano, kill germs, remove toxins, and make a baby all at the same time. And while it's doing that, it tracks the fundamental temporal rhythms that govern the earth and the universe in which it sits. These include circadian rhythms, which are the cyclical beats that measure the biochemical, physiological, and behavioral processes of all living things on earth. They also include seasonal rhythms that have to do with the planet's revolution around the sun and tidal rhythms that have to do with the complex gravitational effects of the sun and moon (lunar rhythms) and other heavenly bodies on our planet and its waters. There are at least a hundred rhythms that chronobiologists talk about. All combined, these compose the pulse than animates our living and breathing cosmos, from the movement of stars and planets, the rotation of the seasons, and the ebb and flow of the oceans and everything else in nature. All of these rhythms are woven into each other with such exquisite correlation that the only reasonable explanation for how it all works is the existence of a deeper intelligence that supports and coordinates it. There exists a conductor to this symphony of the cosmos, and it is the transcendent.

This ultimate supreme genius that pulls all the strings is the stuff that the greatest superheroes (and supervillains) are made of. This intelligence also exists within you, waiting to be identified and engaged with. You engage with it through your sensory experience—seeing, hearing, smelling, tasting, and touching. As you are reading these pages, turn your attention to the one who is doing the reading. That sound you just heard outside your window—ask yourself who is the one who heard it? At every moment as you interact with the world around you, consider the one interacting. That is the real you, a wisp of consciousness taking shape in the world.

Once you begin to see and experience the world as it truly is, as the ceaseless flow of energy and information, *everything* changes. Contrary to some of our great myths, the universe was not created *once upon a time*, but rather is constantly being created and re-created. Superheroes have the ability to stand amid this tempest of change, observe it, and also wield powers that can influence it. We've already reviewed some of those laws (Creativity, Power, Intention), but the ability to express them is grounded in the ability to be rooted in the transcendent state of awareness.

When you consider the infinite improbability of circumstances, synchronicities, miracles, immense seismic energies, and titanic cosmic events that have had to occur to generate this moment, your existence in it, and all of the relationships, experiences, and interactions that make you up, you will come to understand the transcendent. You are the product and culmination of every moment prior to this one—a vast conspiracy of the universe to generate your existence. It's a rather staggering thought, and yet it affirms the reality that your existence is an extension of the universe at large. If any moment before this one had been different, even by the slightest bit, you would not exist as you now know yourself to.

As mentioned, an attribute of the transcendent is its awareness of itself. Borrowing again from Lord Krishna on the battlefield of Kurukshetra, he describes it best when he tells his protégé Arjuna: "I'm going to give you divine eyes, and when I give you divine eyes, you will see the world as it really is." As we have discussed already, although all living things are an expression of consciousness, human beings' unique ability to be self-aware is an extraordinary thing and a quality of the transcendent that expresses itself only through us. We ask ourselves questions no other species does:

Who am I?

Why am I here?

Does my life have meaning and purpose?

What happens to me after I die?

Is there a God? And if so, does she love me?

These are often qualified as spiritual questions. They stem from the existence of our soul, which is just another term for the transcendent. And therein lies the greatest power super-heroes have—a true and intimate connection with their soul. The soul is that state of awareness beneath your senses, the puppeteer pulling the strings and animating that bag of skin and bones or the metaphorical capes and tights that super-heroes wear. It is that presence within you that has always been there—when you were a baby, a teenager, and now.

That presence is truly transcendent—it was there before you were born and will survive your death. Birth and death are simply a parenthesis in the eternal presence of your soul, which does not belong to you any more than it belongs to anyone else. It is a feature of the universal domain that we all belong to.

Your soul is not a thing. It is the potential of all things. Your soul, knowing correlations as it does, is omniscient. Not omniscient in that it has information stored like Wikipedia, but it's intuitive. It's the source of intuition, the source of intention, the source of insight, the source of imagination, the source of creativity, the source of meaning, purpose, and decision making. Your soul co-creates with God, even as it coexists with all of God's creations. In short, the soul is the source of consciousness.

The spiritual traditions of India say that there are seven states of consciousness. The first is the *deep-sleep state*. Even in deep sleep there is some awareness. If, for example, I come, scream at you while you are sleeping, and tell you your house is burning, you'll get up and run. The second state of consciousness is the *dream state*. In the dream state, there exists a level of awareness as well. In fact we construct an entire reality out of it when we are immersed in it. For example, I once dreamed I was in Pebble Beach playing in a golf tournament with Clint Eastwood. I had a magnificent score, beat Mr. Eastwood and everyone else, and walked off with the trophy. Then in the morning when I woke up, I realized that Clint Eastwood, the trophy, Pebble Beach, me, and all the spectators in the gallery—were all me. I manufactured the whole thing in my dream. The dream world is nothing more than a shadow of *real* reality, no matter how real it feels.

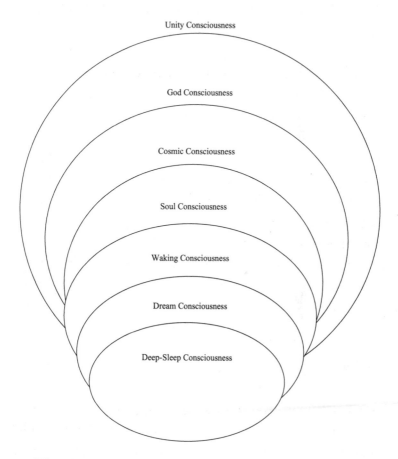

The third state is the *waking state.* However, if you live your waking hours unconsciously, then you are in a "waking dream." There's a story about Buddha that helps us understand the state of awareness that should be present in the waking state.

Lord Buddha is dying. His most devout disciple, Ananda, comes to him, seeking some last pearls of wisdom from his master. He asks Buddha to "tell him who he really is." At first, Buddha keeps quiet.

After a moment, Ananda asks, "Are you God?"

Buddha shakes his head gently and replies, "No."

Ananda speaks again. "Are you a prophet?"

Buddha answers, "No."

Again Ananda queries, "Are you a messiah?"

And again Buddha shakes his head no.

Ananda gets progressively frustrated. "Please tell me—who are you?" he pleads.

And Buddha says, "I'm awake."

That's all we really are, a field of awareness waiting to be woken up. But most people remain asleep, unaware of their real identity. Though they have within them the potential to be a real live superhero, they spend their life stuck in their alter ego, the Clark Kent to their Superman.

The fourth state is *soul consciousness*. Walt Whitman, when he first experienced his soul, said, "I must not be awake, for everything looks to me as it never did before; or else I'm awake for the first time, and all that was before was a mean sleep." Here we are in the midst of that "mean sleep" and are being asked to wake up if we want to get on the path to discovering our true selves. This state of consciousness alerts us to the fact that the prior states of consciousness are illusions.

In the fourth state of consciousness, we begin to sense the deeper reality that is orchestrating the physical world. The veil that separates the physical and spiritual realms begins to tear. Just as we have to wake up from the dream state to experience waking consciousness, we have to wake up from what we call waking consciousness to glimpse our spirit, our inner self. This is called glimpsing and being in touch with the soul.

The fifth state of consciousness is *cosmic consciousness*. In this state, your spirit can observe your material body. Your awareness goes beyond simply being awake in your body, and beyond simply glimpsing the soul, to being awake and alert to your place as part of the infinite spirit. It explains the evangelical catchphrase, "I'm in this world and not of it."

You can observe the body while it's dreaming and simultaneously observe the dream. The same experience occurs in waking consciousness. You have two qualities to your awareness, local and nonlocal, at the same time. Your intuition increases. Your creativity increases. Your insight increases. Because of all of the above, the frequency of so-called coincidences increases.

Cosmic consciousness leads to the sixth state of consciousness, which is *God consciousness*. In this state, the witness becomes more and more awake. You not only feel the presence of spirit in yourself, but you start to feel that same spirit in all other beings. When you look at a grain of rice, not only do you see a single piece of rice, but you also see the farmer who produced it and his ancestors who were and his descendants who will be part of the greater conspiracy that led to his existence. You also recognize in that grain of rice the sunshine, earth, water, wind, and air that conspired to construct it—the whole universe manifesting transiently in a single speck. In recognizing all of this, you're able to fully pierce the mask of reality and feel the presence of God everywhere. In God consciousness, God is not difficult to find—God is impossible to avoid, because there's no way you can go where God is not.

And finally, the seventh state of consciousness is *unity consciousness*. This is also known as "enlightenment." The spirit in the perceiver and the spirit in that which is perceived merge and become one. When this happens, you see the whole world as an extension of your own being, recognizing that there is only one witness to everything and you are that witness. In this state, miracles are commonplace, but they are not even necessary, because the infinite realm of possibility is available at every moment. You transcend life. You transcend death. You are the spirit that always was and always will be.

I remember, many years ago in India, watching a debate between the great teacher Jiddu Krishnamurti and a religious fundamentalist. After quite a bit of back and forth, the fundamentalist looked at Krishnamurti and declared, "You know, the more I listen to you, the more I'm convinced that you're an atheist."

Krishnamurti scratched his head and answered, "I used to be one, until I realized I was God."

This of course, annoyed the fundamentalist. He gasped, "So, you're denying the divinity of Krishna [the Hindu equivalent of Christ]?"

Krishnamurti shook his head vigorously, "Heavens no! I'm not denying him his divinity, nor the divinity of anyone else for that matter!" This is the state we all seek.

The ultimate goal of superheroes is to reach unity consciousness, not intellectually, but experientially. In this experience is infinite power and the ability to heal. And not just heal wounds or even right wrongs, as superheroes are most commonly known to do, but to sway the forces of darkness and maintain the equilibrium the cosmos requires to continue evolving. Superheroes do this by stopping suffering. They understand that there are five principal reasons for human suffering:

1. Not knowing the essential nature of reality.

2. Grasping and clinging to what is ephemeral, transient, and unreal.

3. Being afraid of what is ephemeral, transient, and unreal.

4. Identifying with the socially induced hallucination that is the ego.

5. Fearing death.

We've covered most of these at length in the body of the book, but the fear of death may in fact be the most palpable and familiar. We all look behind ourselves occasionally and see the Prince of Death stalking us. Since the last time we looked, he's a little closer, inching his way toward us. We're all on death row; the only uncertainty is the method of execution and the length of reprieve. So, many of us walk around with this fundamental fear, which is the cause of all other fears: the fear of the unknown. But what if the unknown became known to you? What if you transcended this experience of separation and you knew that there's nothing to fear? What if you really knew yourself as you really are? Who would you be then?

Now more than ever do we need to commune with our transcendent selves—to connect with our souls and embrace our superhero selves. We need not look at the world, see its chaos, and reel back from it; we need to confront it and understand ourselves as citizens of that chaos and masters of it.

In the prior pages, with the help of my son, Gotham, and through the kaleidoscope of some our greatest mythmakers and superheroes, I've attempted to identify and set out some of the most important qualities that enable us to reach our highest potential. I strongly recommend that you read and reread these pages and refine your practice of these laws. It is my belief that it is the path to a more holistic and empowered future—a world that Homer and like minds could only dream of.

As in the pages of the great comic-book stories, the consequence of not pursuing our full potential could be dire.

Turning a blind eye to the full potential of who we can be—and who we really are—risks the fracturing of our collective soul. So that's the brink on which we currently rest, the cusp of an Armageddon of the soul. It's in these times that great heroes rise up to heal our collective wounds. Now you know the skills to be one.

Will you be?

The ability to access the transcendent is the first step toward knowing yourself and reaching your full potential. It is the ability to go inward, beyond the secret passageways, dark alleys, and ghost-filled attics of the mind into pure silence, or Being. Being, after all, is primal and prior to feeling, thinking, and doing. In order to just "be" and experience the infinite field of possibilities, cultivate stillness:

1. *Make mindfulness a part of daily life.* Be mindful of your breath, bodily sensations, sounds, sighs, forms, colors, tastes, and smells. This will manifest as an awakening of heightened sensory experience through attention. The highest form of human intelligence is the ability to observe yourself without judgment.

2. *Practice silent meditation.* The "so-hum meditation" technique is one of the most simple and profound meditation techniques, and you can teach yourself to do it. "So hum" means "I am that." In practicing this meditation, you are essentially reminding yourself

of your base level of existence. To do the so-hum meditation:

Sit in a comfortable position.

Place your hands facing upward on your lap or legs.

Close your eyes and start witnessing your breath.

Observe the inflow and outflow of your breath without trying to control it in any way. (You may find that your breathing spontaneously gets faster or slower, shallower or deeper, and may even pause for a time.)

Observe these changes without resistance or anticipation.

Whenever your attention drifts away from your breath to a sound in the environment, a sensation in your body, or a thought in your mind, gently return your awareness to your breathing.

Introduce the "so-hum" mantra, which is the mantra of breath. Naturally the "so" will align with your inhalation and the "hum" with your exhalation.

Gradually and spontaneously both the mantra and any thoughts will drift away, and you will experience the ground state of consciousness.

Continue this meditation for 15 to 20 minutes or whatever feels comfortable, and then gently draw yourself from it, taking an extra minute or two before you return to normal activity.

3. *Be aware of and intimate with the intelligence of nature* at all times—in leaves and flowers, trees and animals—in every sentient entity. This doesn't mean you have to understand their biology; just appreciate the perfect expression of nature's laws and intelligence in all that exists around you. Nature displays laws and intelligence in action. Take a walk in the park. Go into the wilderness. It's your source. Don't analyze, evaluate, label, judge, or describe. Just observe and be. The intelligence of nature will flow through you.

ACTIVATING THE
SUPERHERO BRAIN

During the past few years, there has been an explosion of new information in the field of neuroplasticity. Neuroscientists are discovering that our brains are not fixed anatomical structures, but very fluid and interconnected processes that embody the flow of energy and information within us, and between us and the outside world. How you think, feel, perceive, and relate constantly influences and alters the so-called structure of the brain. The reason most people appear to have a hardwired brain is that they constantly reinforce the connections through conditioned patterns of thought and behavior.

A quick breakdown of the brain:

- The *prefrontal cortex* (the front part of your brain just behind your forehead) is the part of your brain that makes representations of intention and reflection (among other things).

- The *cortical brain* contains the somatosensory cortex, which makes representations of sensory experience. Herein lie specific dedicated regions, such as the auditory and visual cortices, where representation of sounds and images are made.

- The *motor cortex* of the brain (just in front of the somatosensory cortex) is responsible for executing voluntary movements.

- The *limbic system* is the seat of all emotionality.

- The *reptilian brain* or midbrain, which is a bulbous extension of your spinal cord, is the seat of everything that has to do with survival, including fight-or-flight responses, sleeping and waking cycles, regulation of breathing, balance of chemicals and electrolytes, sexual urges, and other basic instincts.

In other words, for every experience, action, and mode of attention and intention, there is a representation in a specific part of the brain. Superheroes understand this—that sensations, emotions, imagination, and thoughts sculpt and mold the structure of their brains. They can activate through conscious awareness of sensations, emotions, images, and thoughts specific parts of their brains. Therefore, they are mindful of what is going on in their inner life at all times, knowing that it is not only structuring their brain activity, but also reflecting in their outer life. They know that in every moment the world is a reflection of their own state of being.

Through various mental exercises and a mindful life, it is possible to rewire your entire brain. Neurons that fire together, wire together. To summarize:

- Feeling gratitude has the effect of stimulating your limbic brain and fostering nurturing emotions that strengthen self-repair mechanisms and healing. Keep a gratitude journal, or just count your blessings at the beginning or end of every day.

- Meditating on divine attitudes like loving-kindness, joy, and equanimity further enhances the capacity of the limbic system for healing and building healthy relationships.

- Mentally doing a body scan will build the stability of the somatosensory system.

- Visualizing or imagining different sensory modalities stabilizes different parts of the brain that enhance dormant potentials and creativity.

- Physical exercise, including cardiovascular conditioning and weight training, improves the overall functioning of the entire brain.

- Yoga and martial arts enhance mind-body coordination and awaken intuition and creativity.

- Deep and conscious breathing breaks reactive responses.

Let's take this a step farther. The following exercises enable you to rewire your entire brain to help you live a life that is intelligent and creative, has organizing power, and is built on platonic values such as love, goodness, truth, beauty, and evolution. Start with a daily meditation that will further develop the superhero brain:

- Sit quietly in a chair with feet firmly planted on the ground and palms on the lap. Your back should be relatively erect in order to literally elongate the flow of energy through your body.

- Close your eyes.

- Start mentally counting backward from one hundred to zero. Whenever you become distracted, return to wherever you left off. You may hear sounds in the environment or feel sensations in your body. Let them go and gently return to your counting.

- When you reach zero, do a body scan: progressively bring your awareness to your toes, then feet, ankles, calves, knees, thighs, hips, abdomen, chest, neck, face, and head.

- In each of these locations, linger for a few moments and pay attention to any sensations that arise. When they do, ask yourself what the story is behind these sensations. Asking the question is enough. You do not need to hunt for the answers.

- Once you have done the body scan, turn your attention to your breath. Mentally ask it to slow down.

- After two or three minutes, place your attention on your chest and feel your heartbeat either as a sound or a sensation. Ask your heart to slow down.

- Now, keeping your awareness in your heart, evoke emotions as follows:

  Love

  Joy

  Peace

  Equanimity

  Harmony

  Laughter

  Exuberance

  Ecstasy

- You may mentally whisper these thoughts to your heart. If any images come up, pay attention to them.

- Finally, keeping your awareness in your heart, evoke images of great superheroes you admire and observe their compassionate and heroic deeds in your imagination.

- After you are done, relax into your body and open your eyes.

Throughout the day whenever you feel uncentered, become aware of the sensations in the body or breath with eyes open. On occasion place your attention on your heart and ask it to slow down. Remind yourself that you are activating different parts of your brain just by paying attention. Gradually, you will notice activation of your superhero brain.

You can also enhance your sensory experience by practicing the following:

- Practice the so-hum meditation for about five minutes.

- Imagine different sounds: the sound of thunder, a waterfall, a dog barking, a church bell, gunfire, sirens, a child crying. The more you can imagine hearing the sounds of consciousness, the more the neurons in your auditory cortex will fire together and wire together.

- Imagine different sensations: touching the rough bark of a tree, a silk shawl, or a cashmere sweater; digging into the earth with your hands; feeling the sand between your toes as you walk on a beach, the tender touch or kiss of someone you love. There is no end to possible mental experiences.

- Visualize various forms and colors: a red rose, an orange sunset, yellow sunflowers, a green meadow, a blue ocean, an indigo sky.

- Experience tastes in your mind: a sour lemon, ripe strawberries, garlicky Chinese food, chocolate ice cream, the spices of India, mustard, jalapeno, ginger.

- Experience smells in your mind: an Italian kitchen, a pine forest, a favorite perfume or cologne, a locker room in the gym.

By practicing the above, you are cultivating a form of thinking that is multisensory. This will not only enhance your creativity and intuition. It will make your life more vibrant, and you will become alert to the richness and multi-sensory experience of both your inner and outer worlds. Delight of the senses and peak experiences will be more present in all aspects of your life.

Finally, here are ten principles to observe in your daily life that will also help shape your brain by modifying your perception and your behavior:

- For every challenge, the superhero's solution is to go inward.

  Exercise: When faced with a challenge, do not react. Stop, go within, and ask what your creative opportunity is. Live the question until you move into the answer.

- For everything that exists, its opposite also exists.

  Exercise: When faced with a crisis, identify the factors or qualities contributing to it. Focus on the opposite.

- The superhero's perception scans the whole range of existence from smallest of the smallest to the biggest of the biggest.

  Exercise: Look at every object in its wholeness. Know that it is the whole universe localized.

- The superhero is independent of the good and bad opinions of others.

  Exercise: Realize that only the ego thinks in terms of superior or inferior. At the level of being, you are above or beneath no one.

- The superhero never gives in to self-importance.

  Exercise: Do not be offended by people's behavior.

- The superhero takes on the problems of the world.

  Exercise: Ask yourself how you can help, how you can serve.

- The superhero is always aligned with the evolutionary impulse.

  Exercise: In every situation, ask what the greater good is.

- The superhero executes action with impeccability, but is detached from the result.

  Exercise: Focus on the process, not the outcome.

- The superhero is the exquisite combination of dynamic action and stillness of mind.

  Exercise: Even in the midst of chaos and turbulence, be an alert witness to your own actions and reactions.

- The superhero is the best listener in the world.

  Exercise: Listen with your body. Listen with your heart. Listen with your mind. Listen with your soul. Never judge while listening.

Superhero Reading List

Anyone who reads comics knows there's no way to come up with one definitive reading list of the best of them. But it's still a fun game to play.

The following are a dozen modern superhero comics that have something to say about the spiritual laws that drive great superheroes. Please note that this list is limited to modern Western comics and doesn't touch on the incredibly prolific world of graphic fiction that comes out of the rest of the world, notably Japan.

Sequel?

Deepak and Gotham Chopra

Wolverine, by Frank Miller and Chris Claremont
Even the greatest superheroes can't always contain their shadow selves.

Silver Surfer, by Stan Lee and Jack Kirby
Legendary superhero creator Stan Lee identified Silver Surfer as among his favorites. Even though Surfer's epic origin story spans galaxies and transcends time, it's his humanity that makes him one of a kind.

Ex Machina, by Brian Vaughn and Tony Harris

This post–9/11 story explores the ethics, conflicts, and principles that come with being a superhero, not to mention the politics.

Batman: War on Crime, by Paul Dini and Alex Ross

The darkest moments represent a crossroads between creative self-empowerment and total self-annihilation.

Superman: Whatever Happened to the Man of Tomorrow?
   by Alan Moore and Curt Swan

What possibly could have destroyed the world's greatest superhero, Superman? His one vulnerability, kryptonite? His archenemy Lex Luthor? Or the most dangerous of all—his own ego?

X-Men: The Dark Phoenix Saga, by Chris Claremont
   with Dave Cockrum and John Byrne

Real superheroes transcend their own physical form. They don't just tap into the field of infinite power and consciousness; they become it.

Hulk: World War Hulk, by Greg Pak and John Romita Jr.

Empathy and love have the power to populate planets. Vengeance destroys galaxies.

The Invincible Iron Man, by Matt Fraction with Salvador Larroca

In a world fraught with corruption and conflict, creativity is the greatest weapon.

Spider-Man: Kraven's Last Hunt, by J. M. DeMatteis
and Mike Zeck
It's not the roles a superhero plays that define him; it's the role-player beneath the costume he wears that makes him a superhero.

The Death of Captain Marvel, by Jim Starlin
Ironic how it's a superhero's humanity in the face of the most mortal of deaths that really defines his greatest superpower.

All-Star Superman, by Grant Morrison with Frank Quietly
No one knows quantum consciousness like Superman.

Strange, by J. Michael Straczynski and Samm Barnes
The line between science and sorcery is thinner than you think.